Andrew Woods

T0342670

OXFORD GRAMMAR 4

Name: _____

Class: _____

OXFORD
UNIVERSITY PRESS
AUSTRALIA & NEW ZEALAND

CONTENTS

OXFORD UNIVERSITY PRESS

UNIT 1.1 — Common nouns

Under the sea

Common nouns are ordinary nouns that name things, people or places.
Fish, *boat*, *sea*, *shark* and *sailor* are all common nouns.

1 On a separate piece of paper, write three common nouns from the picture opposite that:

a are smaller than you:

b are larger than you:

c are living things:

d are not living things:

e swim:

f float:

2 What am I?

a I have sharp teeth. I have a large, triangular fin on my back. _____

b I am a machine. I sail underwater. _____

c I am a water plant. Sometimes I wash up on the seashore. _____

d I have eight tentacles. When frightened, I can squirt an inky liquid. _____

e I am worn on the face to stop water getting in the eyes. _____

f I am an imaginary sea creature. I am half fish and half woman. _____

3 Underline the words that you think are nouns in each sentence.
(The number of nouns in each sentence is shown in brackets.)

a The shark swam in and out of the shipwreck. (2)

b Beautiful fish hurried past the colourful coral. (2)

c An octopus ignored the submarine as it glided slowly towards the seabed. (3)

d The divers reached the ledge with plenty of air left in their tanks. (4)

Only use a capital letter to begin a common noun if that word begins a sentence.

e High above, a lone dolphin leapt over the buoy. (2)

4 Unjumble these common nouns from the picture.

a ngyoxe knats _____

b kpiwsechr _____

c dmrieam _____

d gihsfni abot _____

CHALLENGE YOURSELF

Use a separate piece of paper or a computer.

Without moving from your chair, can you see and list 50 common nouns?

The Melons' photo album

Honey Dew

Melaneeza

Paddy

Gourdy

Melon Patch

Minnie Lee

Rocky and Walter

Rufus, the Melon Collie

Cantaloupe Lane

Chunky Mellow Chocs

Muskmelon Maulers

River Vine Queen and Cucurbit River

OXFORD UNIVERSITY PRESS

Proper nouns are special names for people, places and things. Proper nouns always begin with a capital letter. For example: *Samir   Katie   Cantaloupe Lane   Friday   Melbourne   October*

1 You can see some photos from the Melon family's photo album opposite. The photos tell us about the lives of the Melons.

For example: *The Melons barrack for the Muskmelon Maulers rugby team.*

Use the photos to help you to make up three statements about the Melons. Remember that proper nouns must begin with a capital letter.

_____

_____

_____

2 Rewrite this sentence, correcting the proper nouns.

Grandma minnie lee melon took her grandchildren, rocky and walter, on a fishing trip along the cucurbit river in her boat, *river vine queen.*

_____

_____

_____

3 Complete this table of proper nouns, using names that begin with the letter that appears at the start of each row.

	Boy's name	Girl's name	Place (town, country, etc.)
M	Mark		
E			Eaglehawk
L			
O		Olga	
N			
S			

4 Circle the words that should begin with a capital letter.

a   My sister anna likes to hear mother goose nursery rhymes before she goes to sleep.

b   "Hey dad!" i called out to my father. "where are you going?"

c   The home of the prime minister, called the lodge, is not far from parliament house.

CHALLENGE YOURSELF

On a separate piece of paper or on a computer, write proper noun place names starting with each letter of your full name. For example: *Mick Smith = Melbourne Inglewood Canberra Kuwait Sydney Maroochydore Ireland Tenterfield Holland*

(Note: If there is an X in your name, the X can be anywhere in the place name.)

Having an idea!

1 _____

2 _____

3 _____

4 _____

5 _____

6 _____

7 _____

8 _____

9 _____

OXFORD UNIVERSITY PRESS

Concrete nouns are the names of things we can see and touch.

For example: *chair, apple, tree, building*

Abstract nouns are the names of ideas and feelings. These things cannot be seen or touched.

For example: *honesty, love, freedom, music*

1 The nouns in the box are abstract nouns. Write them beneath the photos on page 8 that they best match.

love   speed   childhood   sleep   friendship

anger   joy   sadness   envy

The numbers in brackets tell how many abstract nouns are in the proverb.

2 Draw circles around the abstract nouns in these proverbs.

a   Honesty is the best policy. (2)   b   Curiosity killed the cat. (1)

c   Charity begins at home. (1)   d   Strength grows stronger by being tried. (1)

e   Loyalty is worth more than money. (1)   f   Beauty is only skin deep. (1)

3 Change these adjectives or verbs to abstract nouns. For example: *sleepy – sleep*

a   brave _____   b   laugh _____

c   know _____   d   able _____

e   delightful _____   f   silly _____

4 Draw lines to match abstract nouns that are antonyms (opposites).

bravery   deceit

wealth   weakness

strength   success

honesty   poverty

failure   cowardice

CHALLENGE YOURSELF

Write a sentence containing one of these abstract nouns.

opinion, happiness, courage, talent, luck

_____

_____

A strange tale of Viking wives, loaves and elves

Read this story.

Once upon a time — for that is how tales start — there were three Viking wives who baked six loaves. They carefully wrapped the loaves in beautiful silken scarves and placed them carefully upon the shelves of the kitchen.

Passing by were five elves riding magnificent wolves. The elves stole the loaves that the wives had just finished baking.

The wives, with sharpened kitchen knives in hand, climbed onto their spotted calves and chased those thieves.

The elves rode for their lives.

The elves found that they could not outrun the wives so they split the loaves into halves. They hid half under some leaves and the rest they left for the wives to find.

The wives, who were running late for their Viking Wives' Association meeting, said, "Oh well, half a loaf is better than no bread." And on they went with their Viking wives' lives.

OXFORD UNIVERSITY PRESS

To make plural nouns of most words ending in *f* or *fe*, change the *f* or *fe* to *v* and then add *es*.
For example: *elf – elves*   *calf – calves*   *life – lives*

1 Circle the words in the story that have changed from *f* or *fe* to *v* to become plural nouns.

2 Change these nouns to plural nouns.

a loaf _____   b half _____   c wolf _____

d life _____   e wife _____   f scarf _____

g knife _____   h leaf _____   i thief _____

j shelf _____   k self _____   l yourself _____

For some words ending in *f*, just add *s* to form plural nouns. For example: *roof – roofs*

3 Just add *s* to change these nouns to plural nouns.

a chef _____   b chief _____

c reef _____   d cliff _____

e belief _____   f puff _____

Do you remember these plural noun rules? You will need to know them to complete the exercises on this page.
For some words just add s.
For words ending in ch, sh, ss, s or x add es.
For words ending in y following a consonant, change the y to i and then add es.
For words ending in ay, ey or oy just add s.

4 Change the following nouns to plural nouns.

a tiger _____   b marsh _____   c army _____

d gas _____   e cherry _____   f knife _____

g valley _____   h student _____   i leaf _____

5 On a separate piece of paper or on a computer, change each of the following groups of words to plural nouns and then write sentences containing each group.
For example: *leaf, cherry, box*
After we had packed the cherries into boxes, we raked up leaves.
a   monkey, loaf, dish, box   b   city, chimney, life

CHALLENGE YOURSELF

On a separate piece of paper or on a computer, write a short story in which you include the plural nouns of *witch, shelf, thief, key, peach, alley, fairy, journey* and *jelly*.

Harry the Monster
Have you seen him?

IDENTIKIT description:

	head		ears		fangs
	nose		body		skin
	left arm		forearms		waist
	brow		legs		trousers
	claws				

OXFORD UNIVERSITY PRESS

Adjectives tell us more about nouns. They describe things, people, animals and places.
For example: *The tired old man sat with his faithful dog.*
Which words describe the man? (*tired, old*) Which word describes the dog? (*faithful*)
In this sentence, *tired, old* and *faithful* are the adjectives.

1 The monster hunters need to complete their IDENTIKIT picture of Harry. Use the adjectives in the box to complete a description of the wanted monster on the IDENTIKIT form.

floppy	sharp	spotty	furrowed	hairy
bald	thick	hooked	bandy	tattooed
muscular	huge	cuffed	cargo	

*Some words that are usually nouns may also be used as adjectives.
For example: a flower garden, bed covers
Some adjectives are formed from nouns.
For example: anger – angry, taste – tasty, fun – funny*

2 Circle the adjectives that mean the same as the bold words.

a **huge**   gigantic tiny   large   mammoth   enormous

b **thin**   broad   skinny   lanky   plump   slender

c **hooked**   true   crooked curved   straight   bent

d **muscular** feeble   strong   brawny weak   powerful

3 Tick the adjectives that you think best describe Harry the Monster.

☐ gentle   ☐ ferocious   ☐ affectionate   ☐ peaceful   ☐ kind
☐ fierce   ☐ cheerful   ☐ violent   ☐ angry   ☐ jolly
☐ meek   ☐ harmless   ☐ helpful   ☐ dangerous   ☐ wild
☐ vicious   ☐ savage   ☐ friendly   ☐ ruthless   ☐ mean

4 Use adjectives to rewrite these sentences in an improved way.

a   The monster destroyed the village. _____

_____

b   On the table was a feast of sandwiches, fruit, ice cream and lemonade.

_____

_____

CHALLENGE YOURSELF

On a separate piece of paper or on a computer, write as many adjectives as you can think of to describe one of the following: *a winter's day, a summer's day, a dog, a cat, a ride on a roller coaster.*

Five hairy monsters

Five hairy monsters sat down to lunch,
Buttered bits of concrete, munch, munch, munch.
One swats a busy bee sitting on its paw
Falls off his creaky chair, leaving four.

Four savage monsters sat down for tea
Jam on a joke book with roast fiddle-dee.
One starts a-giggling, tee-hee-hee
Laughs himself silly and that leaves three.

Three mean monsters ready for supper
Sawdust and glue and an icy-cold cuppa.
One takes a huge bite and tries to chew
But his jaws get stuck and that leaves two.

Two hungry monsters wake for a feed
Nothing in the pantry so it's agreed —
That those two monsters, each a brother,
Munch on a brekky of one another.

OXFORD UNIVERSITY PRESS

Adjectives are words that describe nouns. Adjectives tell us more about things, people, animals and places. We often expand noun groups by adding adjectives.

1 Which adjectives in the poem 'Five hairy monsters' tell us about these nouns?

a bits of concrete _____

b chair _____

c monsters _____

d bee _____

e cuppa _____

f bite _____

g book _____

h jaws _____

2 Write number adjectives for these nouns. For example: *two arms*

a _____ monsters

b _____ paws

c _____ chair legs

d _____ days (in a week)

3 Match the adjectives describing nationality with the nouns in the box.

dragon   bagpipes   kimono   boomerang   elephant   pyramids

a Scottish _____

b Australian _____

c Chinese _____

d Japanese _____

e Egyptian _____

f African _____

4 Underline the noun groups and colour the adjectives in these sentences.

a The fierce bushfire was brought under control by the brave, hard-working firefighters.

b Tammy was a naughty dog for chasing the frightened sheep.

c Deep in the wild woods, the slumbering dragon stirred from his long sleep at the sound of the huge explosion.

5 Change these nouns to adjectives that can be found in the poem.

a hair _____

b butter _____

c hunger _____

d ice _____

CHALLENGE YOURSELF

On a separate piece of paper or on a computer, rewrite these sentences using adjectives to expand the noun groups, making them more interesting.

On the street, the trams and cars are like insects before a storm.

The tiger stalked the goat through the jungle.

Welcome to Country

Have you ever been to an important event like a special celebration or a sporting grand final? If you have, then before the event started you may have seen and heard a Welcome to Country.

A Welcome to Country might involve dancing, music or a smoking ceremony (in which native plants are smouldered to produce smoke which wards off bad spirits from the people and the land).

The most important part of a Welcome to Country is spoken by an Elder from an Aboriginal or Torres Strait Islander community.

There are many Aboriginal and Torres Strait Islander communities across Australia. Each community has boundaries around their traditional lands. The boundaries are not fences or walls or lines marked on a map. They are the mountain ranges and waterways — the natural features of our land. When someone wants to cross into the traditional land of an Aboriginal or Torres Strait Islander community, they are given permission in the form of a Welcome to Country.

The traditional land of the Wurundjeri people is the land around Melbourne. Aunty Joy Murphy is an Elder of the Wurundjeri people. She is often asked to perform a Welcome to Country on behalf of her people.

OXFORD UNIVERSITY PRESS

1 Circle the noun groups in these sentences from the Welcome to Country text on page 16.

    a Have you ever been to an important event like a special celebration or a sporting grand final?

    b There are many Aboriginal and Torres Strait Islander communities across Australia.

    c The traditional land of the Wurundjeri people is the land around Melbourne.

Remember, a noun group usually contains an adjective and a noun.

2 Write four proper nouns that have been used in the text on page 16.

_____   _____

_____   _____

3 Write adjectives from the 'Welcome to Country' text to complete these noun groups.

    a _____ ranges   **b** _____ features

    c _____ celebration   **d** _____ lands

    e _____ plants   **f** _____ spirits

4 Change the following common nouns to plural nouns.

    a boundary _____   **b** community _____

    c ceremony _____   **d** country _____

CHALLENGE YOURSELF

Write an abstract noun from the box that might name a feeling or idea to match the following sentences.

> delight   bravery   pride

a What Aunty Joy Murphy is feeling as she performs a Welcome to Country

_____

b How you might feel if your team is playing in a grand final _____

c What a surf lifesaver might show as she enters the ocean to rescue a struggling swimmer _____

TOPIC 1: TEST YOUR GRAMMAR!

Nouns, adjectives and noun groups

1 Shade the bubble next to the common noun.

○ gigantic   ○ villain   ○ swam   ○ silently

2 Shade the bubble next to the correct plural noun for **knife**.

○ knifes   ○ knifies   ○ knivies   ○ knives

3 Shade the bubble next to the proper noun.

○ manager   ○ Wilson Street   ○ mountain   ○ giraffe

4 Shade the bubble next to the concrete noun.

○ kindness   ○ despair   ○ factory   ○ humour

5 Shade the bubble next to the abstract noun.

○ cry   ○ sorrow   ○ unhappy   ○ sad

6 Shade the bubble below the abstract noun in this sentence.

The children's enthusiasm for the project astonished Mrs Bryant.

   ○   ○   ○   ○

7 Shade the bubble next to the correct plural noun for **fairy**.

○ fairys   ○ fairies   ○ faires   ○ faireys

OXFORD UNIVERSITY PRESS

8 Shade the bubble next to the type of noun represented by these naming words.

talent, mercy, skill, intelligence

○ common   ○ proper   ○ abstract   ○ concrete

9 Shade the bubble below the adjective in this sentence.

We had to hold on to our hats in the gusty wind.

○   ○   ○   ○

10 Shade the bubble next to the word that can be used as a noun or an adjective.

○ safe   ○ chilly   ○ safely   ○ narrow

11 Shade the bubble next to the adjective.

○ think   ○ wild   ○ blew   ○ write

12 Shade the bubble next to the noun group that contains an adjective.

○ an enchanting story   ○ a diamond   ○ an elephant   ○ the sunset

TICK THE BOXES IF YOU UNDERSTAND

Common nouns are ordinary nouns that name things, people and places. ☐

Proper nouns are special nouns for people, places and things. ☐

Concrete nouns name things we can touch and see. ☐

Abstract nouns are names for ideas and feelings. ☐

Many nouns must change to form plural nouns. ☐

Adjectives describe nouns. They can be used with nouns to form noun groups. ☐

Verberella

Poor Cindy spends her days mopping, scrubbing, wiping, dusting, washing, vacuuming, polishing and daydreaming.

She dreams that one day she will become The Girl of Steel Wool – Verberella!

Verberella leaps over tall buildings.

She blows fire from her mouth.

She flies like a jet-fighter.

She lifts boulders with one hand and then smashes them with the other hand.

She tosses bad guys aside.

Most importantly of all, she does the housework very, very quickly.

OXFORD UNIVERSITY PRESS

Doing verbs tell us what is being done in a sentence. They tell us about the action.
For example: *The whale swam. I heard them arrive.*
What did the whale do? *It swam.* What did I do? *I heard. Swam* and *heard* are doing verbs.

1 Read 'Verberella' and find doing verbs that could fill the gaps in these sentences.

a Verberella _____ over tall buildings.

b Verberella _____ boulders with one hand.

c With her other hand Verberella _____ boulders.

d Verberella _____ like a jet-fighter.

e She _____ bad guys.

f She _____ her housework quickly.

g She _____ fire from her mouth.

2 Rewrite these words as doing verbs by adding the ending *ing*.

a (Just add *ing*.) dust _____, wash _____,

toss _____, vacuum _____, polish _____

b (Double the last letter.) mop _____, cut _____,

clap _____, scrub _____, rub _____

c (Drop the final *e*.) wipe _____, bite _____,

ride _____, race _____, wriggle _____

3 Write six doing verbs that tell us what Cindy does and six doing verbs that tell us what Verberella does.

Cindy _____

_____

Verberella _____

_____

Some words can be verbs or nouns. For example: I am washing. I hung out the washing. I wish I was famous. I made a wish.

CHALLENGE YOURSELF

On a separate piece of paper or on a computer, write 20 doing verbs that tell us something about the way different parts of your body act.
For example: *my toes wriggle, my eyes stare, I clench my fist*

Danny Verb

Danny Verb has a new skateboard.

He dresses in his tough jeans and long-sleeved shirt.

Danny pulls on his helmet.

He slides into his boots.

He checks and then puts on his elbow pads.

Danny buckles on his kneepads.

Finally, Danny slips in his mouthguard.

Just as well because ...

Danny takes a tumble!

OXFORD UNIVERSITY PRESS

Verbs tell us what is happening or being done in the sentence.
For example: *Danny skates down the road.*
What does Danny do? *Danny skates.* (*Skates* is the verb.)

1 Read 'Danny Verb' on page 22 then underline the doing verbs below that tell us what is being done.

    a Danny buckles on his kneepads.   **b** Danny slides into his boots.

    c He checks his elbow pads.   **d** Danny slips in his mouthguard.

    e Danny takes a tumble.   **f** He pulls on his helmet.

Sometimes verbs can be more than one word. We call these verb groups.
For example: *was running, is skating, are sliding*

2 Look around your classroom and write down three sentences containing two-word verbs that tell what people are doing. Underline the verb groups in your sentences.

For example: *Jason **is sitting** at his table. Nick and Carmel **are talking**.*

_____

_____

_____

3 Match the occupations with their most likely verbs. For example: *A pilot flies.*

Occupations	Verbs
mechanic	serves
author	operates
waiter	repairs
surgeon	sells
salesperson	plays
musician	writes

When *having* or *being* words are used on their own, we call them relating verbs.
Having words: *had, have, has.* Being words: *am, are, is, was, were, will, shall, be.*
For example: *The skateboard **is** on the shelf. Danny **has** kneepads. I **am** here. We **are** happy.*

4 Write the sentence from the comic strip that contains a relating verb.

_____

5 Choose a relating verb from the box above and write it in a sentence of your own.

_____

CHALLENGE YOURSELF

Create a verb poster by collecting images of actions and then labelling the pictures with verbs.

Limericks

A scientist named Ted Maclean
Invented a time machine
Took a trip to the past
Said, "I'm sure this won't last."
Then vanished and has not been seen.

Matilda from Woolloomooloo
Liked to bathe in a product called Gloo
But she ran out of luck
One day and got stuck
On the fur-lined seat of her loo.

Now Brian from Bendigo
Instead scrubbed himself with Velcro
He'd rubbity-dub
And scrubbity-scrub
'Til his mum cried, "Where'd that boy go?"

An Australian player of old
His name being Warne I am told
Once let go a flipper
A rippety-dipper
And found himself out! Cleanly bowled!

OXFORD UNIVERSITY PRESS

Saying verbs are verbs that show the manner in which something is being spoken or has been spoken.
For example: *giggled, replied, groaning, says, said*

1 Read 'Limericks' and look for clues to help you circle the saying verbs in these sentences.

a "I'm sure this won't last," said Ted.

b "Help, I'm stuck!" screamed Matilda.

c "Where'd that boy go?" cried Brian's mum.

d I was told the player's name was Warne. (Be careful!)

Remember,
a verb can be made up
of more than one word.

2 Write suitable saying verbs from the box in the sentences below.

> asked   sighed   shouted   groaned   suggested   laughed

a "I'm bored!" _____ Rupert.

b "Where'd you buy your new backpack?" _____ Samantha.

c Mr Costanza _____ for the boys to paddle back to the beach.

d "Not maths again!" _____ the children.

e The audience _____ hysterically at the comedian's punchline.

f "Why don't you turn it around this way?" _____ the science teacher.

3 Select three of the following saying verbs and, on a separate piece of paper or on a computer, write sentences of your own.

> giggled   complained   growled   replied
> whispered   cried   yelled

CHALLENGE YOURSELF

Read this well-known limerick and then circle the saying verb in it.

An epicure dining at Crewe
Found a rather large mouse in his stew.
Cried the waiter, "Don't shout
And wave it about,
Or the rest will be wanting one too!"
(An epicure is a person with refined taste in food and drink.)

Dog at school

OXFORD UNIVERSITY PRESS

Thinking and feeling verbs show what we think, believe or feel about things. They commonly express an opinion on something.

For example: *"I know what I'll do next,"* **thought** *Briana.*

We **like** *to ride our bikes after school.*

1 Read the comic strip, then use the thinking and feeling verbs from the box to complete the sentences.

> decided   pretend   wondered   persuade   thought

a Wal couldn't _____ Dog to come to work today.

b Dog _____ he had learnt a lot at school.

c Wal _____ where Dog was hiding.

d "I'll _____ I can't hear Wal," _____ Dog.

2 Draw circles around the thinking or feeling verbs in these sentences.

a Do you believe in fairies?

b The scientist concluded that climate change was a reality.

c "I think I'll have the orange one," decided Ahmed.

d "My son likes tennis," said Mrs Banner.

> Thinking and feeling verbs are sometimes called sensing verbs.

3 Use three of the thinking and feeling verbs below to write sentences of your own.

love, hate, felt, trust, enjoy

_____

_____

_____

CHALLENGE YOURSELF

Write three things you might wish for if you had a magic lamp.

In each of your sentences, use the thinking and feeling verb **wish**.

_____

_____

_____

Wendy's time bubble travel map

yesterday

when I was young

last Friday   flew

when I will be very old

The past

was sailing

explored

was flying

THE FUTURE

It was

later

next year

were

next century

will fly

I was

It will be

will sail

lived

I will be

then

tomorrow

will

will live

is sailing

is living   I am

is flying

will explore

The present

now

explores

this minute   It is

at the moment

today

are

OXFORD UNIVERSITY PRESS

Verbs can show us whether something has happened (past), is happening (present) or will happen (future). We call this the verb tense.

1 Read 'Wendy's time bubble travel map' and then add the correct verb tense to complete the table.

Past	Present	Future
I was	I am	I _____
_____	_____	will live
flew	is sailing	_____
_____	_____	_____
_____	explores	_____

The word tense comes from the Latin word *tempus*, meaning 'time'. When we talk about the tense of a verb, we are talking about the time that the action in the sentence has taken place.

2 Write whether these extracts from Wendy's diary are about the past, present or future.

a   I am adjusting the MT4ME button. It needs a twist and a wrench. _____

b   We will arrive in ten minutes. I will send my robot cats X-Port and M-Port out of the

bubble first. _____

c   We landed on the deck of the *Endeavour*. I met Captain Cook and Banks and found

them to be pleasant and intelligent men. _____

3 Change these sentences to the past tense.

a   I am drinking my milkshake. _____

b   The cat will creep slowly towards the unsuspecting bird. _____

_____

4 Change these sentences to the present tense.

a   I will throw the basketball to you. _____

b   The dancers came onto the stage. _____

_____

CHALLENGE YOURSELF

Imagine some of the things Wendy might see and do on her time-travelling journeys. Using 'Wendy's time bubble travel map', write three sentences in her diary (use a separate piece of paper or a computer). Write one sentence about the past, one about the future and one about the present. What things would you do if you could travel in a time bubble?

Scorch

YOU might be feeling TIRED AND LISTLESS!

YOU could be low on energy levels!

YOU may need a pick-me-up!

Perhaps YOU would benefit from a NEW, exciting, healthy drink

... if so, then ...

... YOU should drink SCORCH

SCORCH – it will certainly perk up YOUR day!

Scorch is definitely made from all-natural ingredients: 100% water!

OXFORD UNIVERSITY PRESS

Some verbs help us to express ideas about what is possible. These verbs are called modal verbs.
For example: *might, may, can, will, ought to, could, should, would, need to*

1 Read the advertisement for 'Scorch' to help you complete these sentences with modal verbs.

a   You _____ benefit from a new drink.

b   You _____ be feeling tired.

c   Scorch _____ certainly perk up your day.

d   People who are low on energy levels _____ enjoy Scorch.

e   For an exciting and healthy drink you _____ drink Scorch.

> Modal verbs are never used alone. They are helping (auxiliary) verbs.

Modal adverbs are words that tell us to what degree something will or won't happen.
For example: *I probably won't watch television tonight. It's possibly going to rain tomorrow.*

2 There are three modal adverbs in the advertisement on page 30. Write them on the line below.

_____

3 Draw circles around the modal verbs in these sentences.

a   I might go to the movies tonight.

b   "You should take an umbrella with you," suggested Seth.

c   "You must have a good memory," said Mrs Banner.

4 Select a modal adverb from the box and write it in a sentence.

> obviously   apparently   arguably   possibly   hardly   definitely

_____

_____

CHALLENGE YOURSELF

Persuasive texts such as the advertisement for 'Scorch' often use the pronouns *you, us* or *we* to include and appeal to the audience. With a partner, write a short advertisement on a separate piece of paper or on a computer. Include the pronouns *you, we* or *us* and some modal verbs and adverbs.

The adventures of Adverb Man

The train slowly leaves the station.

Soon it is rumbling quickly through the countryside.

The train speeds onwards!

WHOOSSHHHH

But not far down the track

the bridge has collapsed suddenly!

The passengers chat happily!

The train rapidly approaches the bridge!

The passengers are unaware of the fate that awaits them soon!

This looks like another job for ADVERB MAN!

Adverb Man carefully assesses the situation.

Train rumbling quickly!

Bridge collapsed suddenly!

Passengers chatting happily!

Their fate awaits them soon!

WOOO SSSSHHHHHH

He flies swiftly to the scene.

Using his power of E L O N G A T I O N, Adverb Man stretches himself across.

He has bravely become a human bridge!

Another job heroically done, Adverb Man!

OXFORD UNIVERSITY PRESS

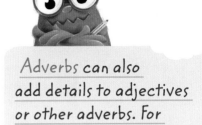

Adverbs add details about verbs. For example: *She writes neatly.*
Many adverbs end in *ly* (*quickly, carefully*) but some don't (*later, here, fast*). Adverbs often tell *how, when* or *where*.
For example: *The boat glided* **slowly**. (How did the boat glide? *slowly*)
The train is arriving **later**. (When is the train arriving? *later*)
The rabbit stopped **here**. (Where did the rabbit stop? *here*)

> Adverbs can also add details to adjectives or other adverbs. For example: She is a really neat writer. OR She writes really neatly.

1 Underline the adverbs in these sentences from the story of Adverb Man.

   a   The train slowly leaves the station. (Ask: *How does the train leave?*)

   b   Soon it is rumbling quickly through the countryside. (Ask: *How is the train rumbling?*)

   c   The bridge has collapsed suddenly. (Ask: *How or when has the bridge collapsed?*)

   d   The train speeds onwards. (Ask: *Where does the train speed?*)

   e   The passengers chat happily. (Ask: *How?*)

   f   The train rapidly approaches the bridge. (Ask: *How?*)

   g   The passengers are unaware of the fate that awaits them soon. (Ask: *When?*)

   h   Adverb Man stretches across the gap. (Ask: *Where does Adverb Man stretch?*)

2 Use adverbs from the story that tell us more about Adverb Man.

   a   How does Adverb Man assess the situation? _____

   b   How does Adverb Man fly to the scene? _____

   c   How does Adverb Man become a human bridge? _____

   d   How does Adverb Man complete another job? _____

3 Write an adverb from the box that can be used to replace the underlined group of words below. For example: *We crossed the road* **with great care**. (carefully)

> peacefully   softly   easily   here   quietly   soon

   a   The thieves approached the doorway <u>in a quiet way</u>. _____

   b   She answered the question <u>in a soft voice</u>. _____

   c   Mark and Irene will arrive <u>in a short while</u>. _____

   d   The baby slept <u>in peace</u> throughout the violent hailstorm. _____

   e   The watch was found <u>in this place</u>. _____

   f   Harvey won the race <u>with ease</u>. _____

CHALLENGE YOURSELF

On a separate piece of paper or on a computer, write adverbs that tell how you do these things:
run, work, sleep, walk, swim, climb, play

Preppo Boy returns

From his lookout above his hideout Preppo Boy spots trouble.

A billy-cart is speeding down a steep slope and seems to be headed straight for a tree.

Quick as a flash, Preppo Boy is on the scene. With nerves of steel he stands in the path of the hurtling cart.

He stops the cart just before the tree. Another cart rushes past the tree.

In billy-cart number 7 is a very angry Nicky Woops.

In billy-cart number 5 is the winner of this year's Fantastic Billy-Cart Downhill Derby — a very happy Dom Blamey.

Isn't she great!

She's the best!

She's wonderful!

Wasn't she fast!

In the sky and flying faster than a speeding bullet to his hideout is Preppo Boy — with a very red face.

OXFORD UNIVERSITY PRESS

Prepositions are small connecting words. Prepositions connect nouns, pronouns or phrases to other words within a sentence.

For example: *The girl is* **on** *the swing.*

The word *on* tells us where, and it connects the girl and the swing.

1 Here is a list of the most common prepositions. Circle the 11 prepositions from the list that are also in the story about Preppo Boy.

about	around	between	into	past	above	at
by	near	through	across	before	down	of
to	after	below	for	off	towards	against
beside	from	on	under	along	beneath	
over	until	up	upon	with	in	

2 Use prepositions to complete these phrases from the story.

a _____ billy-cart number 5

b _____ nerves of steel

c _____ a tree

d _____ his lookout

e _____ his hideout

f _____ the path

g _____ the tree

h _____ the scene

i _____ a steep slope

j _____ the sky

k _____ his hideout

l _____ a very red face

Sometimes two prepositions are used together. For example: away from, down into, along with

3 Underline the prepositions in each sentence.

a The cat climbed over the fence.

b We were asked to wait until the bell rang.

c The billy-cart hurtled towards the tree.

d She left her umbrella near the doorway.

e The boats passed between the flags and headed into the bay.

f The homeless children slept under the bridge.

CHALLENGE YOURSELF

On a separate piece of paper or on a computer, rewrite the sentences below as many times as you can, giving them a different meaning by changing only the prepositions.

For example: *The jar was on the table. The jar was under the table.*

The billy-cart crashed beside a tree.

We ate pizza during the show.

She jumped into the creek.

The robber ran along the road.

The Moon

The Moon has a face like the clock in the hall;
She shines on thieves on the garden wall,
On streets and fields and harbour quays,
And birdies asleep in the forks of the trees.

The squalling cat and the squeaking mouse,
The howling dog by the door of the house,
The bat that lies in bed at noon,
All love to be out by the light of the Moon.

But all of the things that belong to the day
Cuddle to sleep to be out of her way;
And flowers and children close their eyes
Till up in the morning the sun shall arise.
                    Robert Louis Stevenson

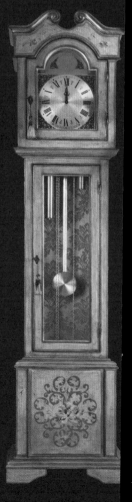

OXFORD UNIVERSITY PRESS

Phrases are groups of words without verbs. Phrases help to make sentences more interesting. Phrases tell us when, where and how. Phrases that begin with a preposition are called prepositional phrases.

For example: *The wind howled. The wind howled **during the night**.* (when)
*The wind howled **through the open window**.* (where) *The wind howled **with frightening force**.* (how)

1 Use the poem 'The Moon' to help you underline the prepositional phrase in each of these sentences and write whether it tells **when**, **where** or **how**.

a The clock was in the hall. _____

b The bat sleeps at noon. _____

c The birdies sleep in the forks of trees. _____

> *Phrases can come at the end, at the beginning or in the middle of sentences.*

2 Complete the sentences below using prepositional phrases from the box.

> in an angry voice   in the morning   on the classroom display board

a We pinned our projects _____.

b The bus will be departing _____.

c The giant demanded more food _____.

3 Complete the sentences below using prepositional phrases from the box.

> Beside the swaggie   Near the council offices   Without hesitation

a _____ the lifesaver plunged into the raging surf.

b _____ the protestors stopped and waved their signs.

c _____ walked his faithful dog, Blue.

4 Underline the prepositional phrases in these sentences.

a My alarm clock always rings at six o'clock.

b We saw a very funny clown at the circus.

c Three possums sat on the leafy branch munching the fruit.

CHALLENGE YOURSELF

On a separate piece of paper or on a computer, write your own phrases to complete the sentences.

a We followed   b The horse cantered   c The storm struck

Somali food

Is ka warran!

In the Somali language that means 'Hello' and 'How are you?'

My name is Najaha. My family came to live in Australia five years ago. Let me share some of my favourite Somali meals with you.

For breakfast my family eats *angero* or *muufo*. They are homemade pancakes. Sometimes we might fry some *bur*, which are doughnuts made from flour, coconut milk powder, yeast, sugar and cardamom.

Lunch is the main meal of the day for my family.

We are a Muslim family so we only eat *halal* meals (*halal* means that the food can be eaten according to our Islamic religion). We do not eat pork products like ham or bacon. Our lunch may be goat meat, chicken or fish with rice or even pasta.

For a snack, we occasionally eat *sambusas*, which are pastries filled with meat, onion, herbs and spices.

On special food occasions, such as Eid, which we celebrate at the end of our fasting month of Ramadan, we eat treats. My favourite is when we make *halwa*. *Halwa* is a very sweet treat. It tastes delicious, so whenever it is served we gobble it up greedily.

OXFORD UNIVERSITY PRESS

1 Underline the doing verbs in these sentences about the text on page 38.

    a My family came to live in Australia five years ago.

    b For breakfast my family eats *angero* or *muufo*.

    c Whenever *halwa* is served we gobble it up greedily.

2 Circle the saying verbs in these sentences.

    a "My name is Najaha," said the young girl.

    b "Do you fast for the whole month of Ramadan?" asked the journalist.

    c "It tastes delicious!" exclaimed Najaha.

3 Use the text on page 38 to help you write adverbs to complete the following sentences.

    a We _____ eat *halal* meals.

    b It tastes delicious, so _____ it is served we gobble it up _____.

    c For a snack, we _____ eat *sambusas*.

4 Underline the prepositional phrases in these sentences.

    a A huge dish of *halwa* was placed upon the table.

    b In the distance we could see the parade of circus entertainers marching around the bend.

    c People of many different cultures have settled throughout Australia.

CHALLENGE YOURSELF

On a separate piece of paper or on a computer, write sentences about food containing these thinking and feeling verbs.

wonder   *imagine*   *enjoy*   *dislike*

TOPIC 2: TEST YOUR GRAMMAR!

Verbs, adverbs and prepositional phrases

1 Shade the bubble next to the doing verb.

○ crept   ○ hero   ○ quietly   ○ spider

2 Shade the bubble below the doing verb in this sentence.

A thief stole the precious diamonds from the museum.

○ ○ ○ ○

3 Shade the bubble below the relating verb in this sentence.

The suitcase with the red ribbon was on the carousel.

○ ○ ○ ○

4 Shade the bubble next to the saying verb.

○ laughed   ○ walked   ○ sat   ○ is flying

5 Shade the bubble next to a saying verb that could complete this sentence.

Sergeant Wilson ⬭ *for volunteers.*

○ ran   ○ slept   ○ asked   ○ thought

6 Shade the bubble below the feeling verb in this sentence.

Melanie loves to ride her horse Misty.

○ ○ ○ ○

7 Shade the bubble next to the sentence that is in the past tense.

○ I am holding the cup.   ○ I will hold the cup.

○ I might hold the cup.   ○ I held the cup.

OXFORD UNIVERSITY PRESS

8 Shade the bubble beneath the modal verb in this sentence.

We might go to the Royal Melbourne Show on Tuesday.

○   ○   ○   ○

9 Shade the bubble next to the adverb.

○ walked   ○ upon   ○ eagerly   ○ bright

10 Shade the bubble below the adverb in this sentence.

We should take an umbvrella because it will possibly rain.

○   ○   ○   ○

11 Shade the bubble next to the prepositional phrase in this sentence.

Cass and Rob are riding their bikes to school.

○ Cass and Rob   ○ are riding   ○ their bikes   ○ to school

TICK THE BOXES IF YOU UNDERSTAND

Doing verbs tell us what is being done, has been done or will be done. ☐

Saying verbs show us the manner in which words are spoken. ☐

Thinking and feeling verbs show what we think, believe or feel about things. ☐

Verbs can show us tense – past, present and future. ☐

Modal verbs and adverbs express ideas about what is possible. ☐

Adverbs tell us more about verbs. ☐

Prepositional phrases are groups of words beginning with a preposition and without a verb that tell us when, where and how. ☐

UNIT 3.1 Text cohesion – antonyms

Busy Anto Nym

1

Anto Nym works for a circus. His busy day begins at dawn when he unloads the circus truck. Up goes the big tent for the show and up goes the little tent where the performers change.

2 Anto Nym's next job is to advertise the show and sell tickets. He does this by dressing as a clown and riding his 'Crazy Bike' through the town. He wears a serious face but he performs funny tricks. Many people buy tickets because they think Anto is funny.

3

At dusk, Anto Nym shows people to the entrance of the big tent.

4 Anto is an acrobat. He performs on the trapeze where he swings up and down.

5

Anto also juggles. He tosses and catches many objects at the same time. He makes juggling look easy when it is really very difficult.

6 Later Anto helps to form a human tower with his brothers Syno and Hommy. Anto is on the top and Hommy, the strongest of the brothers, is on the bottom.

7

Late at night, when the performance has finished, Anto shows people to the exit and then he relaxes until bedtime.

8

As the week ends, down comes the little tent and down comes the big tent. Anto then loads everything onto the circus truck. He makes sure that nothing is left behind and then he drives to the next town.

OXFORD UNIVERSITY PRESS

Antonyms are opposites. For example: *on/off afternoon/morning peace/war*

1 Find words in the story on page 42 that are antonyms for these words.

a loads _____ b big _____ c serious _____ d up _____

e entrance _____ f day _____ g begins _____ h begun _____

i bottom _____ j dawn _____ k tosses _____

l idle _____ m easy _____ n buy _____

2 Add the prefixes *un-*, *dis-* or *mis-* to make the following words antonyms.

a _____ agree b _____ fair

c _____ fold d _____ fire

e _____ believe f _____ hurt

g _____ behave h _____ kind

i _____ prepared j _____ known

k _____ approve l _____ real

> Many *antonyms* can be formed by adding a *prefix* or changing the *suffix*. For example: *unhappy, invisible, misunderstood, disobey, impossible, illegal, careful/careless, useful/useless*

3 Unjumble the words in the box to make antonyms for the words below.

> tcupaer   stew   gtubho   fots   yrd
> eefzre   lmlas   wef   hirgt   rsuqea

a boil _____ b sold _____

c firm _____ d escape _____

e many _____ f large _____

g moist _____ h left _____

i east _____ j circular _____

CHALLENGE YOURSELF

Write antonyms for the following words by changing the suffix.

a meaningful _____ b cheerful _____

c hopeless _____ d thoughtless _____

Syno Nym, the acrobat

Presenting Syno Nym the trampolining acrobat …

Syno goes up and

Syno rises and

Syno ascends and

Syno comes down.

Syno drops.

Syno soars and

Syno climbs and

Syno descends.

Syno dives.

Syno falls.

And everyone goes home with cricks in their necks.

Ow!   Ow!   Ouch!   Oh!   Mummy, my neck hurts!

OXFORD UNIVERSITY PRESS

Synonyms are words that mean the same (or nearly the same) as other words.
For example: *big – large, huge, great, massive;*
sad – unhappy, glum, gloomy, depressed

> It is a good idea to build up a word bank of synonyms as a reference to improve your writing. When you write a simple word such as **big**, think, "Are there better words that mean the same or nearly the same?"

1 Use the story on page 44 to help you write synonyms for:

a goes up _____

b comes down _____

2 Circle the word in each group that is NOT a synonym for the bold word.

a	**happy**	glad	cheerful	sad	jolly	delighted
b	**strong**	powerful	muscular	mighty	feeble	robust
c	**costly**	expensive	pricey	cheap	valuable	dear
d	**bad**	evil	nasty	naughty	wicked	good
e	**fast**	rapid	speedy	quick	slow	swift

3 Replace the underlined word in each sentence below with a synonym from the box.

> tidy   famous   difficult   savage   wandering
> damp   free   purchased   roads   village

a Robbie's towel was still <u>wet</u> _____ from the sudden downpour.

b The rock star had become <u>well known</u> _____ in only a short time.

c Hector was asked to leave his room <u>neat</u> _____ before going out.

d We <u>bought</u> _____ our new television at the market on the corner.

e Mrs Mackie told us that the test would not be <u>hard</u> _____.

f A <u>wild</u> _____ tiger was <u>loose</u> _____ and

roaming _____ around

the <u>streets</u> _____ of our <u>town</u> _____.

CHALLENGE YOURSELF

On a separate piece of paper, match the words in Box A with their synonyms in Box B.

A
messy	hoax	dawn
small	odour	select
old	kind	banquet
sharp	ascend	weary
minimum	new	

B
tired	least	choose
trick	generous	pointy
smell	ancient	modern
feast	morning	untidy
climb	tiny	

Homonymbus ~~Won~~ One

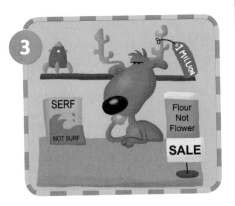

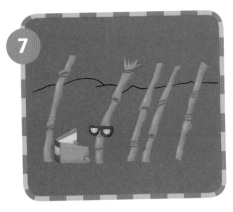

OXFORD UNIVERSITY PRESS

Homonyms are words that sound the same but have different meanings.
For example: *sun* (the Earth's star) *son* (a male child)
stake (a stick with a point) *steak* (a thick piece of meat)

1 Write the numbers of the pictures on page 46 that best fit these phrases or sentences.

a   A dear deer _____   b   That's a foul fowl! _____   c   A bare bear _____

d   The nose knows _____   e   A boy on a buoy _____   f   A cheap cheep _____

g   A leek with a leak _____   h   What does a reed read? _____

i   A thrown throne _____   j   Which witch won one? _____

2 Underline the correct homonyms in each sentence.

a   The children were not (aloud / allowed) to play (their / there) music (aloud / allowed) during (their / there) lunch (break / brake).

b   Ms Sanchez (read / red) a (tale / tail) about a monkey with a magical bright (read / red) (tale / tail).

c   The artist painted the (seen / scene) as she had (seen / scene) it on her recent trip to the outback.

d   At the (fair / fare) we were asked to (sell / cell) tickets for people to visit the (sell / cell) in which Ned Kelly had (been / bean) imprisoned.

> Homonyms can be *homographs*, words with the same spelling but different meaning, for example: bear (animal), bear (to carry), or *homophones*, words with the same sound but spelt differently and with different meanings, for example: pear/pair, blue/blew.

3 Write homonyms that mean the following:

a   the time after the sun sets _____; a medieval soldier in armour _____

b   hurt _____; a sheet of glass for a window _____

c   a small stream _____; a sharp squeaking sound _____

CHALLENGE YOURSELF

On a separate piece of paper or on a computer, draw one of the following:
- A mussel with muscles up to his/her waist in waste OR
- Patients losing patience while waiting to lose weight OR
- A three-toed toad being towed behind something with a sail that is for sale.

Tides

Have you ever battled to get a sandcastle finished at the beach before it is swamped and washed away by a rising tide? We often incorrectly say that tides 'come in' and 'go out' but in fact tides rise and fall. What is it that causes tides to rise and fall?

The Moon is the main culprit responsible for the movement of tides all over Earth. Being the closest body to Earth in space, the Moon exerts a strong gravitational pull on our planet. The gravitational pull of the Moon causes the oceans on Earth to bulge towards it. At the same time, Earth itself turns around the Sun and there is a gravitational pull between them. The constant forces at work in these two orbits mean that when the Moon causes water to bulge towards it on the side of Earth nearest to the Moon, it also causes an equal bulge on the other side. This means, strangely, that when there is a high tide on one side of the planet there is also a high tide on the other side.

Wherever you are on the coast, there will be a high tide every 12 hours and 25 minutes, and therefore two high tides every 24 hours and 50 minutes. This is because Earth rotates a full 360° in 24 hours (that's one complete rotation per day). In the same 24 hours, the Moon rotates 12° around the Earth.

So, to be a successful sandcastle builder, it's best to begin your castle at low tide and finish it within 12 hours and 25 minutes.

OXFORD UNIVERSITY PRESS

We use paragraphs to organise the information we write. A paragraph is a section in a piece of writing that begins on a new line and deals with a single idea or theme. Paragraphs usually start with a topic sentence, which tells us the main point of the paragraph.

1 Number the paragraphs in the information report on page 48 from 1 to 4 so that you can use those numbers to answer the questions that follow.

    a Which paragraph tells us what causes tides? _____

    b Which paragraph introduces the information report? _____

    c Which paragraph explains how often we have high tides? _____

    d Which paragraph contains a concluding statement? _____

2 Write the sentence from paragraph 2 that you think is the topic sentence.

_____

_____

_____

_____

CHALLENGE YOURSELF

'Tides' is an explanation. Explanations tell why things happen or how something works or has formed. Explanations are organised into paragraphs. Another type of informative text, an information report, also uses paragraphs to organise information into bundles.

    On a separate piece of paper or on a computer, write an information report about an animal of your choice.

Organise your writing into paragraphs that cover these areas:

- Introduce and classify your animal: What kind of animal is it? Which animal family does it belong to? Is it a mammal, a reptile, a bird, a domestic/tame animal?, etc.

- What does it look like?

- Where do you find it?

- What does it eat?

- Your last paragraph should be a concluding statement.

Raven and the magician

Once, long ago, the Sun was kept prisoner in a secret box in the house of a cruel magician. Raven wanted to free the Sun, so he went to the house where the Sun was kept. He saw that the magician's daughter went to the same place at the stream to drink and bathe each day.

Raven used his magic to change himself into a baby. He placed himself in a reed basket close to the stream.

When the magician's daughter came to the stream she was tricked. She fell in love with the baby and took him home with her.

In the disguise of the baby, Raven started to cry. He cried and he cried and he cried. The magician's daughter brought toy after toy for the baby but he would not stop crying.

Finally, the magician could stand no more. He told his daughter to let the baby play with the Sun.

This was the chance that Raven had been waiting for. He quickly changed back to his bird form and, gripping the Sun tightly, he flew up the chimney of the magician's house.

The magician was very angry. He made the flames leap up high after Raven. The flames burnt Raven and turned his beautiful white coat to the black we know today.

The magician would not give up the Sun easily. He turned himself into a hawk and flew after Raven.

Raven knew he was no match for the fast-flying magician, so he broke off some slices of the Sun and threw them back for the magician to catch. Instead, these slices spread about the sky and became the stars.

Still the magician chased Raven.

Raven broke off a large piece of the Sun and threw it at the magician. The magician ducked and that piece of the Sun became the Moon.

Finally, Raven decided that he could not escape the magician while he was carrying the Sun, so he hurled her far into the sky where she has shone brightly ever since.

adapted from a Native American folk tale

OXFORD UNIVERSITY PRESS

Pronouns can stand in the place of nouns to make sentences easier to read.
Some of the most common pronouns are: *he, she, it, his, himself, him, her, herself, hers, I, me, mine, yours, ours, theirs, themselves, ourselves, we, myself, you, its, itself, them, they.*

1 Read 'Raven and the magician', then rewrite the following sentences, replacing the underlined nouns with pronouns.

a Raven wanted to free the Sun, so Raven went to the house where the Sun was kept.

_____

_____

> *Never use an apostrophe with the pronoun its. (It's is a contraction of it is.)*

b When the magician's daughter came to the stream, the magician's daughter was tricked. The magician's daughter fell in love with the baby and took the baby home with the magician's daughter.

_____

_____

c Raven was tired so Raven broke off some slices of the Sun and threw the slices of the Sun back for the magician to catch.

_____

_____

Pronouns that show us that someone owns something are called possessive pronouns.
The most common possessive pronouns are: *mine, ours, yours, his, hers, theirs.*

2 Write possessive pronouns from the box below that best fit into the gaps in the sentences.

> theirs   ours   mine   yours

a This bag belongs to you. This bag is _____.

b That pencil belongs to us. It is _____.

c The pet rabbit belongs to me. It is _____.

d Mr Carver judged the model show. He told the boys that he liked _____ best of all.

CHALLENGE YOURSELF

On a separate piece of paper or on a computer, write a paragraph with four sentences about yourself. Include the pronouns *I, me* and *mine* in your paragraph.

Ancient Greek gods

Zeus, who was the chief god, often became angry with humans. He hurled lightning bolts that would shake the Earth.

Hera, who was the wife of Zeus, sometimes tried to help humans.

She often repaired the damage that the bad temper of Zeus had caused.

Another violent god was Ares, who was the god of war. Ares loved to start battles and wars, which sometimes lasted for years.

Apollo was a handsome god who loved music and archery.

It was Apollo who drove the sun-chariot that lit up the sky and gave the world daylight.

Athena, who was the goddess of wisdom, was the daughter of Zeus. Athena was another god who tried to protect humans.

She looked after some humans by giving them special powers that helped them to conquer monsters.

Poseidon, the god of the seas, had the power to start earthquakes. He carried a weapon called a trident that could stir up the oceans until they caused terrible and furious storms.

Hades, whose name means 'the unseen one', was the god of the underworld. The underworld was a place for the dead, guarded by the three-headed dog Cerberus, who would stop the dead from returning to the land of the living.

OXFORD UNIVERSITY PRESS

Who, which and that can also be used as pronouns.

These pronouns can be used to tell us about a person or thing already mentioned in the sentence.

For example: *Zeus, who lived on Mount Olympus, threw frightening lightning bolts.*

These pronouns can also be used to join two sentences.

For example: *Another violent god was Ares. Ares was the god of war.*

⟶ *Another violent god was Ares, who was the god of war.*

Who has taken the place of *Ares* to save us repeating that name.

1 Use the pronouns **who** (or **whose**), **which** or **that** to write these pairs of sentences as one sentence. The text opposite will help you.

a Apollo was a handsome god. Apollo loved music and archery.

_____

b Poseidon carried a trident. The trident could stir the oceans into terrible and furious

storms. _____

_____

c Ares loved to start battles and wars. The battles and wars sometimes lasted for years.

_____

d Hades was the god of the underworld. Hades' name means 'the unseen one'.

_____

e Hera was Zeus's wife. Hera tried to help humans.

_____

Who refers to people. *Which* or *that* are generally used to refer to things, animals and plants.

2 Finish these sentences in your own words.

a My neighbour, who _____ .

b I saw a horse that _____ .

c We caught the train, which _____ .

d The boy who _____ .

CHALLENGE YOURSELF

On a separate piece of paper or on a computer, rewrite these sentence pairs as single sentences, using either *who* or *that* to join them.

a I borrowed a library book. It was all about building model aeroplanes.

b We met a lady. She had just arrived in Australia from Turkey.

c Taz showed me the house. It was thought to be where a wizard lived.

Yoghurt crunch

Here's a delicious breakfast recipe that can also double as an 'any time' snack.

1 cup rolled oats

1 tbsp light olive oil

2 tbsps maple syrup

1/3 cup blanched almonds, chopped

1/3 cup pecans, chopped

1/3 cup chopped dried apples

1/3 chopped dried apricots

yoghurt to serve

Rolled oats

Olive oil

Maple syrup

Method

1   First, preheat the oven to 180°C.

2   Place the rolled oats in a medium bowl and drizzle with olive oil and maple syrup, then stir to combine.

3   Next, spread the oat mixture over a baking tray and bake in the oven for 5 minutes.

4   Now sprinkle the almonds and pecans over your oat mixture, then bake for 5–7 minutes, stirring once during the cooking process. When the nuts are golden brown and crisp, transfer the oat mixture to a bowl to cool.

5   When cool, stir in the dried apples and dried apricots.

6   Finally, sprinkle the mixture over your favourite yoghurt and enjoy! (Serves 6)

Dried fruit and nuts

Yoghurt

Yoghurt crunch

OXFORD UNIVERSITY PRESS

When words are used to sequence events, steps in a recipe or arguments, these words are called text connectives. Text connectives form links between sentences or paragraphs.
For example: **First** fold the paper in half, **then** write your name on one half. **Next** fold the paper in half again. **Finally**, place the paper in an envelope.

1 Read the recipe on page 54, then circle the text connectives in the sentences below.

a First, preheat the oven to 180°C.

b Finally, sprinkle the mixture over your favourite yoghurt and enjoy!

c Place the rolled oats in a medium bowl and drizzle with olive oil and maple syrup, then stir to combine.

d Next, spread the oat mixture over a baking tray and bake in the oven for 5 minutes.

e Now sprinkle the almonds and pecans over your oat mixture, then bake for 5–7 minutes, stirring once during the cooking process.

2 Use time sequence text connectives of your own to complete these sentences. If you need help then you will find some text connectives in the Challenge Yourself box below.

a _____ we put on our socks and boots.

b _____ we went outside to play.

c To _____ with, I placed the ball on the ground, _____ kicked it as hard as I could towards the goal.

d My little brother had several turns and _____ he kicked a goal too.

e _____ my friend Jack showed us how to make a mark.

f _____ we are going to ride our bikes to the park.

CHALLENGE YOURSELF

Here is a list of some text connectives.
first, to begin with, to start with, first of all, for a start, next, now, then, soon, later, afterwards, meanwhile, finally, to conclude, in conclusion, last
On a separate piece of paper or on a computer, write out a recipe or set of instructions using text connectives to help the reader follow the recipe in the correct order.

Fascinating food facts

Did you know that honey can never go 'off'?
The acids in honey help to keep bacteria out. In fact, edible
honey was found in the Ancient Egyptian pyramids. Despite
the honey being thousands of years old, archaeologists
found that it could still be safely eaten.

If you eat large amounts of carrots, your
skin will eventually turn orange. However,
there is no evidence to suggest that eating
lots of carrots will allow you to see well in
the dark.

Roman soldiers were often paid in salt.
In fact, the word 'salary' comes from
the Latin word for 'salt' – sal.

Almonds are eaten as nuts, although
they are actually members of the
peach family, and are therefore fruits.

You can test whether an egg is 'off' by
placing it in a bowl of water. As the egg
ages, gas builds up inside the shell, making
the egg buoyant. Because of this, the
egg will float in water and this signals that
it should not be eaten.

There are about 100 000 bacteria in just
1 litre of drinking water. Nevertheless,
water is essential and we should aim to
drink 6 to 8 glasses every day.

The first canned food was invented in
1804 to feed Napoleon Bonaparte's army.
The can opener, however, wasn't invented
until 48 years later.

OXFORD UNIVERSITY PRESS

Text connectives are a way of showing the reader how the text is developing or what is coming up. They can link ideas together.

For example: *Hippos appear to be slow, friendly animals. However, they are among the most dangerous creatures on Earth. (However is the text connective, because it links two ideas.)*

1 Read the text on page 56 to help you fill in the missing text connectives.

a The acids in honey help to keep bacteria out. _____, edible honey was found in the Ancient Egyptian pyramids. _____ the honey being thousands of years old, archaeologists found that it could still be safely eaten.

b Almonds are eaten as nuts, _____ they are actually members of the peach family, and are therefore fruits.

c There are about 100 000 bacteria in just 1 litre of drinking water. _____, water is essential and we should aim to drink six to eight glasses every day.

d As an egg ages, gas builds up inside the shell, making the egg buoyant. _____, the egg will float in water and this signals that it should not be eaten.

e The first canned food was invented in 1804. The can opener, _____, wasn't invented until 48 years later.

> Text connectives can be confused with conjunctions. However, conjunctions can only be found within sentences, whereas text connectives form links between sentences or even paragraphs.

2 Text connectives can differ in their function. Circle any text connectives below that could sequence time.

first	therefore	later	however
otherwise	soon	for example	finally
nevertheless	in fact	earlier	in any case

CHALLENGE YOURSELF

Circle the words below that you think form the two text connectives in these sentences.

The hare is an extremely fast animal. On the other hand, the tortoise is a very slow reptile. All the same, in Aesop's famous fable, the tortoise was victorious in its race with the hare.

Strange parade

Last night I had the strangest dream
As odd as it could be.
I dreamt I was a gildfosh
Sitting in a tree.
And as I sat upon a limb
Sipping lemonade,
A weird procession passed me by –
An animal parade.

First there came two kongarees
    upon their heads were crowns.
Followed by three parrokots
    in chequered dressing gowns.
Then came four clomping lozrads
    their feet encased in boots.
Behind them strode five pussims
    in prickly prison suits.
Next prancing down the laneway
    six fregs in underwear
And seven bonnie bunyoops
    in wigs of long blonde hair.

Then came a feathered tiger sneak
And she did hiss to me,
"Now come on down and join the gang
From out that old gam tree."
Well how could I resist her?
That wicked, sneakish charmer.
So down I hopped and joined the troop
All in my plastic armour.

OXFORD UNIVERSITY PRESS

Authors often use word play to make their writing more interesting and entertaining. Some authors use nonsense words.

1 Read 'Strange parade', then write sensible nouns for these nonsense words from the poem.

a gildfosh _____

b kongarees _____

c parrokots _____

d lozrads _____

e pussims _____

f fregs _____

Another type of play on words is the pun. A pun is a word play in which a word or phrase is used in a different way to make what is being written humorous.
For example: *I used to be a tailor but I found the work was just so-so.*

2 Write the endings from the box that best fit these puns.

> they're two-tyred   Go on ahead and I'll follow on foot! free of charge
> Then it hit me!   He got twelve months!   Eventually it came back to me.

a I wondered why the baseball bat was getting bigger. _____

b Flat batteries were given out _____.

c Did you hear about the thief who stole a calendar? _____

d What did the shoe say to the hat? _____

e I couldn't remember how to throw a boomerang. _____

f Bicycles can't stand up on their own because _____.

Authors also use word play such as spoonerisms. A spoonerism is a word play in which the first letters or sounds of words are mixed up.
For example: *It's a lack of pies. (It's a pack of lies.) Wave the sails! (Save the whales!)*

3 Can you identify these fairy tale spoonerisms and write them correctly?

a The Pea Little Thrigs

b Beeping Slooty

c The Prog Frince

CHALLENGE YOURSELF

With a partner, read the poem again, taking turns to replace the nonsense words listed in question 1 with some of your own.

Unbearable! (but funny)

Read these rather strange sports comments:

1 He's a player not blessed with vertical height.
Cricket commentator — Michael Slater

2 PENRITH PANTHERS POUNCE ON PADDY
Headline on sports pages

3 "The road ahead to the finals is as straight as an arrow," said the basketball coach.

4 "Let me sew you to your sheet," said the MCG steward at the start of the game.

5 "Wham! Bang! That's another smash from Sami!" shouted the excited commentator.

6 "He's like a shark without a notion!"

Surfing commentator

OXFORD UNIVERSITY PRESS

When we write, we can use language devices to make our writing interesting, entertaining and even funny.

Write numbers to match the following language devices and their explanations with the strange comments on page 60.

A I am a pun. A pun is a humorous play on words which have similar sounds but different meanings. _____

B I am a tautology. A tautology is when there is an unnecessary repetition of words. A tautology contains words that say the same thing. _____

C I am alliteration. Alliteration is the repeated use of the same initial letter or sound in a group of words. _____

D I am a spoonerism. A spoonerism is a sentence in which sounds or parts of words have been mistakenly switched in such a way as to make the sentence humorous.
_____

E I am a simile. A simile is a group of words that liken one thing to another. _____

F Onomatopoeia is the use of words that, when read, sound like the sound they are describing. _____

CHALLENGE YOURSELF

Can you draw lines to match the pun joke with its punchline?

A

Have you ever tried eating a clock?

What did the knife and fork say to the salad?

I couldn't remember how to throw a boomerang

I used to have a fear of the first hurdle

I knew a joke about amnesia

What does a clock do when it is hungry?

B

Lettuce begin.

but I eventually got over it.

It goes back four seconds!

It's time consuming!

but then it came back to me.

but I forgot how it goes.

TOPIC 3: TEST YOUR GRAMMAR!

Text cohesion and language devices

1 Shade the bubble next to the antonym for **tame**.

○ time   ○ domestic   ○ wild   ○ happy

2 Shade the bubble next to the antonym for the underlined word in this sentence.

We walked towards the theatre entrance.

○ doorway   ○ exit   ○ cafe   ○ entry

3 Shade the bubble next to the prefix that can be added to **behave** to make an antonym for this word.

○ un-   ○ dis-   ○ im-   ○ mis-

4 Shade the bubble next to the prefix that can be added to **obey** to make it an antonym.

○ un-   ○ dis-   ○ im-   ○ mis-

5 Shade the bubble next to the synonym for **weak**.

○ feeble   ○ strong   ○ powerful   ○ fortnight

6 Shade the bubble next to a synonym for the underlined word in this sentence.

The interior of the building had been beautifully decorated.

○ outside   ○ hallway   ○ inside   ○ entrance

7 Shade the bubble next to the pronoun that can be used to take the place of the noun group underlined in this sentence.

Andy took his old bike out of the shed and rode the bike to school.

○ his   ○ them   ○ it   ○ him

OXFORD UNIVERSITY PRESS

8 Shade the bubble below the pronoun in this sentence.

Mr Lewis tried to repair the bike but he didn't have the right tools.

9 Shade the bubble next to the pronoun that could replace the noun group underlined in this sentence.

The boys decided to catch the bus but the boys didn't have enough money.

○ them   ○ you   ○ we   ○ they

10 Write text connectives to correctly fit the time sequence in the following.

_____ crack the eggs into a bowl.

_____ whisk them for a minute or two.

_____ pour them into a small frying pan.

_____ cook them for three minutes _____ serve on toast.

11 Shade the bubble next to the text connective that could be used to link the following sentences.

Nate was only a young lad. _____, he had yet to turn 10 years old.

○ Instead   ○ At least   ○ Otherwise   ○ In fact

TICK THE BOXES IF YOU UNDERSTAND

Antonyms are opposites. ☐

Synonyms are words that mean the same or nearly the same. ☐

Homonyms are words that sound the same but have different meanings. ☐

Pronouns can stand in the place of nouns. ☐

Language devices can be used to make our writing more entertaining. ☐

Singenpoo vs Mungo

… The competition continued for another three rounds. All with the same result. The judge called out the score. "Mungo seven. Singenpoo none."

This was terrible. We were going to lose. What was wrong? What, what, what? Singenpoo looked dizzy and upset. She was staggering around in circles.

Just then I noticed something. Mr Spock was beckoning to me. I jumped down from the stage and he whispered in my ear while Mungo was having his next turn.

I stared at Singenpoo. Then at the writing on the board.

"So that's it," I said.

I rushed over to Singenpoo and took off my glasses. Then I fixed them on Singenpoo's head by bending the arms behind her ears. "Try these," I said. "The writing is too small for you to read."

Singenpoo really looked funny wearing glasses, but she started purring. Everybody laughed.

Now maybe she would be able to read the words. Maybe we still had a chance. Just maybe.

I looked at the word on my next card. Or rather I didn't look at the word on my next card. They were just a blur. Now I couldn't read them. Nothing was going right.

I raced over to Mum. "Can I borrow your glasses?" I said. Mum handed me her glasses and I stared through them at the next word on my list.

ELEPHANT
ELECTRIC

"Elephant," I said. Singenpoo walked straight over and dabbed at ELEPHANT.

Mum and Singenpoo's fans in the audience went wild. They stamped and cheered like crazy.

"Dinghy," said Mr Cane. Mungo walked up and down, staring at the blackboard. In the end he put a paw on the word DOUGH. Everyone was quiet. Mungo had made his first mistake.

Now it was Singenpoo's turn to show what she was made of. Now that she could see properly she started to get words right. And Mungo began to make errors. The bulldog couldn't read any words with silent letters in them like COMB or KNIFE. Gradually Singenpoo started to catch up.

from *Singenpoo Strikes Again* by Paul Jennings

OXFORD UNIVERSITY PRESS

A **sentence** is a group of words that make sense on their own.

A sentence must begin with a **capital letter** and end with a **full stop**, a **question mark** or an **exclamation mark**.

A sentence can be in the form of a statement. For example: *I stared at Singenpoo.*

A sentence can be in the form of a question. For example: *What was wrong?*

A sentence can be in the form of an exclamation. For example: *So that's it!*

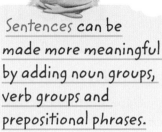

Sentences can be made more meaningful by adding noun groups, verb groups and prepositional phrases.

1 Tick the groups of words below that are **sentences**.

a at the writing on the board ☐

b This was terrible. ☐

c DOUGH ☐

d We were going to lose. ☐

e Mr Spock beckoning ☐

f Can you see Singenpoo? ☐

g Everybody laughed. ☐

h said ☐

2 Complete these **sentences** from the story of Singenpoo.

a They stamped and cheered _____

b Gradually Singenpoo _____

c "Can I borrow _____

d _____
_____ but she started purring.

3 Make up your own **sentences** using these beginnings.

a On Tuesday _____

b What are you _____

c Help, I'm _____

4 Make up your own **sentences** using these endings.

a _____ at the supermarket on the corner.

b _____ on your holidays?

c _____ for your lives!

CHALLENGE YOURSELF

On a separate piece of paper or on a computer, write or type five **sentences** that describe an animal without using the name of the animal. Make sure you write about how the animal moves as well as its appearance. Let a friend read your sentences and try to identify your animal.

The fisherman and the bottle

There once was a fisherman who was very poor.

One day he was casting his net for fish as he usually did.

Upon his first cast, he drew from the sea only seaweed and shells. He was very disappointed. His second cast drew only sand and mud from the sea. Again, he was disappointed. The fisherman cast his net a third time and when he drew the net from the sea he saw that once again he had caught no fish. He was about to give up when a strange object caught his eye. Trapped in a corner of the net was a bottle.

"I wonder what this could be?" he asked himself. He looked closely at the bottle. He found that it had been shut tightly up with lead. He shook the bottle but heard nothing. The fisherman took his sharp fish knife and cut the lead from the neck of the bottle. He turned it upside down and shook it, but nothing came out. He set the bottle down on the sand and as he stood staring curiously at it something strange began to happen.

Slowly a thick blue smoke started to rise out of the neck of the bottle. The smoke spread out over the water and began to take the shape of a gigantic genie.

The fisherman trembled with fear.

"Who are you?" he stammered.

"Bow to me before you die!" roared the genie.

"But please, great master, tell me, who are you?" said the frightened fisherman.

"Bow before you die!" bellowed the genie once more.

"Why must I die?" asked the fisherman. "Have I not set you free? Should I not be rewarded rather than punished?"

"I cannot allow you to live," said the genie. "During my first one hundred years of imprisonment in that bottle I vowed that the person who released me would be made rich beyond their wildest dreams. In my second century trapped in the bottle I grew bitter and I vowed that whoever released me would feel my wrath and die. Therefore, little man, prepare to die!"

"Since I am to die," said the poor fisherman, "may I ask one final question?"

"Ask!" yelled the genie.

"Were you really in that bottle? You are huge and the bottle is tiny. I cannot believe that you could fit into it."

"That bottle was my prison for two hundred years. Of course I can fit into it!"

"Then prove it to me, oh great one," cried the fisherman.

The genie instantly changed himself into smoke and disappeared into the bottle.

The fisherman quickly jammed the lead back into the neck of the bottle.

"Let me out!" pleaded the genie.

"You will kill me if I release you," said the fisherman.

"Oh please let me out!" begged the genie. "I promise no harm will come to you. In fact, I will grant you any wish you desire."   **To be continued …**

OXFORD UNIVERSITY PRESS

A statement tells us something. Statements begin with a capital letter and end with a full stop.
For example: *There once was a fisherman who was very poor.*
A question asks something. For example: *Have I not set you free?*
An exclamation is a short sentence said with strong feeling.
Exclamations begin with a capital letter and end with an exclamation mark.

1 Finish these statements, questions or exclamations from the story.

a   Of course I _____

b   The fisherman trembled _____

c   Why _____

d   Let me _____

e   Were you really _____

2 Write complete statements to answer these questions.

a   Why did the fisherman tremble with fear? _____

_____

b   How long had the genie been trapped inside the bottle? _____

_____

3 Write questions to match these statements.

a   The fisherman used his fish knife to open the bottle. _____

_____

b   Thick blue smoke started to rise from the bottle. _____

_____

4 In the speech bubble write an exclamation of your own that you might make to warn someone about a possible danger.

CHALLENGE YOURSELF

The story of the fisherman and the bottle is unfinished. On a separate piece of paper or on a computer, finish the story in your own words. Include statements, and at least one question and one exclamation.

Occupations

solve crimes.

Bakers

fly aeroplanes and helicopters.

The butcher

bake bread and cakes.

Pilots

sells meat.

A carpenter

make and alter clothes.

Architects

A jockey

writes books.

Detectives

Journalists

rides horses in races.

Florists

design buildings.

An author

makes things with wood.

flies into space.

Tailors

sell flowers.

An astronaut

write for newspapers and magazines.

OXFORD UNIVERSITY PRESS

Do you remember?

The subject of a sentence tells us who or what the sentence is about.

For example: *The birds chattered in the treetops.* (Who chattered? *The birds*)

The verb tells us about the action or feelings in a sentence.

For example: *The birds chattered in the treetops.* (What did the birds do? *Chattered*)

Subjects and verbs in the same sentence must agree.

For example: *Frogs croak.* ✓   *Frog croak.* X   *The frog croaks.* ✓   *The frogs croaks.* X

  The children are playing. ✓   *The children is playing.* X

1 Use the page opposite to help you write sentences to match the occupations of the people with the jobs they do.

a   Bakers _____.

b   An author _____.

c   Pilots _____.

d   A carpenter _____.

e   A jockey _____.

f   Tailors _____.

g   Architects _____.

h   Journalists _____.

i   Detectives _____.

j   The butcher _____.

k   An astronaut _____.

l   Florists _____.

To agree, a singular subject must take a singular verb, and a plural subject must take a plural verb.
For example: The dog is barking loudly. The dogs are barking loudly.

A helping verb is also called an auxiliary verb.

2 Circle the correct helping verb to agree with the subject in each sentence.

a   The cats (is/are) sleeping on the verandah.

b   Timmy and Mary-Lou (was/were) running to the train station.

c   The red balloon (has/have) popped.

CHALLENGE YOURSELF

On a separate piece of paper or on a computer, rewrite or type the following sentences correctly.

a   Sheep was grazing in the paddock.

b   The birds is flying north for the winter.

c   My team are the best.

d   My best friend were waiting at the bus stop.

The beach

The beach was yellow sand, but at the water's edge a rubble of shell and algae took its place. Fiddler crabs bubbled and sputtered in their holes in the sand, and in the shallows little lobsters popped in and out of their tiny homes in the rubble and sand. The sea bottom was rich with crawling and swimming and growing things. The brown algae waved in the gentle currents and the green eel grass swayed and little sea horses clung to its stems. Spotted botete, the poison fish, lay on the bottom in the eel-grass beds, and the bright-coloured swimming crabs scampered over them.

On the beach the hungry dogs and the hungry pigs of the town searched endlessly for any dead fish or sea bird that might have floated in on the rising tide.

from The Pearl by John Steinbeck

OXFORD UNIVERSITY PRESS

Conjunctions are joining words. Conjunctions can join words that are the same kind. For example, two nouns, two adjectives or two prepositions.

For example: *in **and** out*   *small **but** strong*

1 Use the conjunction **and** to join words from the box to make phrases.

> safe   up   Jill   sound   sweet   Jack   down   sour

_____

_____

2 Use the conjunction **but** to join words from the box to make phrases.

> | untidy | slow | clean | not forgotten |
> | sure | gone | happy | tired |

> **Remember**
> that **and** is not the only conjunction (joining word). Don't make your writing boring by overusing the word **and**.

_____

_____

3 Use a conjunction to join these word pairs from the story.

a rubble _____ sand   b shell _____ algae

c bubbled _____ sputtered   d fish _____ sea bird

Coordinating conjunctions (*and, but, so, or*) can be used to join simple sentences together to form longer, compound sentences.

4 Rewrite these sentences using the coordinating conjunctions **and** and **but** to join them.

a Fiddler crabs bubbled and sputtered in their holes in the sand. In the shallows little lobsters popped in and out of their tiny holes in the rubble and sand.

_____

_____

b The beach was yellow sand. At the water's edge a rubble of shell and algae took its place.

_____

_____

CHALLENGE YOURSELF

On a separate piece of paper or on a computer, complete these compound sentences in your own words.

a I hate basketball but ...   b ... and rode off at a gallop.

c The boat is sinking so ...   d ... but I wasn't scared.

Con Junkshun, the fruit and vegie man

My name is Con and I am a greengrocer. I sell fruit and vegetables.

I sell my fruit and vegetables in boxes and in crates.

I buy my fruit and vegetables from farmers in the country and I only buy good-quality produce.

Being a greengrocer is hard work but I enjoy my job.

My produce is always fresh so my customers go away satisfied. They say, "That Con Junkshun has a great stall. He knows it is important to stock only fresh fruit and vegies or people will shop elsewhere."

I wake up very early so I am always at the market before opening time, at dawn.

At 4:30 a.m. a truck arrives from the country and I use my forklift to unload the fresh produce.

On Sunday mornings I don't work at the market so I have time to cook breakfast for Mrs Junkshun and all my little bambino Junkshuns.

OXFORD UNIVERSITY PRESS

Conjunctions are joining words.

Conjunctions can join words. For example: *fruit and vegetables*

Conjunctions can join phrases. For example: *in boxes and in crates*

Conjunctions can join two or more sentences to make one sentence.

For example: *I wake up very early. I am always at the market before opening time, at dawn.*

I wake up very early so I am always at the market before opening time, at dawn.

1 Read about Con Junkshun on page 72, then use coordinating conjunctions from the box to join the sentences below.

> and   but   so

a   I sell fruit. I sell vegetables. _____

b   My name is Con. I am a greengrocer. _____

_____

c   Being a greengrocer is hard work. I enjoy my job. _____

_____

d   My produce is always fresh. My customers go away satisfied. _____

_____

e   At 4:30 a.m. a truck arrives from the country. I unload the produce. _____

_____

f   On Sunday mornings I don't work. I have time to cook breakfast for my family.

_____

2 Underline the coordinating conjunction in each compound sentence.

a   Lions roar but cats meow.

b   I love going to the market and I am sure you will love it too.

c   I might go for a walk today or I might ride my bike.

d   On the way to school the car broke down so we were late.

e   A greengrocer sells fruit and a butcher sells meat.

CHALLENGE YOURSELF

On a separate sheet of paper or on a computer, write or type a few sentences telling what you would do if you had incredible superpowers. When you have finished, circle all the conjunctions in your writing.

Robin the Not-so-good

OXFORD UNIVERSITY PRESS

We cannot always use speech bubbles to show speaking. When writing, we use quotation (speech) marks to show that words are being spoken.

For example: *"What time is it?" asked Roger.*

The words actually spoken by Roger are *What time is it?*

These words begin and end with quotation marks.

Use quotation marks to show words that are actually being spoken. This is called quoted speech or direct speech).

1 Fill the gaps with the words spoken by the characters in the comic strip on page 74.

"_____

_____

_____," said Robin.

"_____?" asked the peasant.

"_____

_____," answered Robin.

"_____

_____!" shouted the peasant.

"_____ !" said Robin.

2 Add quotation marks before and after the quoted (direct) speech in these sentences.

a   Put that down now! shouted Mr Robran.

b   Could someone help me take down the tent please? pleaded Maree.

c   Life wasn't meant to be easy, moaned Uncle Phil as his boat began to sink.

d   Stop! commanded the sentry. No one may enter without a special pass.

3 Add quoted (direct) speech to complete these sentences.

a   The phone rang so I picked it up and said, _____

_____.

b   On the last day of school we all ran through the school gate

shouting, _____.

CHALLENGE YOURSELF

Record a 30-second conversation with one of your friends and then, using quotation marks where necessary, write your conversation down.

Matilda and the Gorilla

Indirect speech

Matilda was out walking when she met an enormous gorilla. She took the gorilla to a police station and asked what she should do with the hairy beast.

Matilda was told by a police officer that she should take the gorilla to the zoo.

The next day the police officer saw Matilda walking down the street with the gorilla.

He asked why she hadn't taken the animal to the zoo as he had suggested.

Matilda told the officer that she had indeed taken the gorilla to the zoo and today she thought she would take him to the movies.

Direct speech

Matilda was out walking when she met an enormous gorilla. She took the gorilla to a police station.

"What should I do with this hairy beast?" she asked a police officer.

"Take him to the zoo," said the police officer.

The next day the police officer saw Matilda walking down the street with the gorilla.

"Why didn't you take that gorilla to the zoo?" asked the police officer.

"Oh, I did take him to the zoo," said Matilda, "and today I thought that I would take him to the movies."

OXFORD UNIVERSITY PRESS

Quoted (direct) speech and speech bubbles show the words that are actually spoken.

For example: *"Where are you going?" asked Tam.* The words actually spoken are *Where are you going?* The speech marks around these words show that they are the exact words spoken.

Reported (indirect) speech is a report of what has been said. For example: *Tam asked me where I was going.* There is no need for speech marks because we are not writing the exact words used by Tam.

1 Fill the gaps with the exact words spoken from the story. Remember to include quotation marks (speech marks) where they belong.

_____

_____ Matilda asked the police officer.

_____said the police officer.

_____he asked.

_____said Matilda,

_____

_____

2 Rewrite these indirect speech sentences as quoted (direct) speech.

For example: *Benny asked how much my bike cost.*
  "How much did your bike cost?" asked Benny.

a The old woman told me that it was six o'clock.

_____

b Petra said that she was sorry that she was late for the start of the game.

_____

3 Rewrite these direct speech sentences as reported (indirect) speech.

For example: *"Who's been eating my porridge?" asked Papa Bear.*
                  Papa Bear asked who had been eating his porridge.

a "I'll huff and I'll puff and I'll blow your house down," shouted the wolf.

_____

b "Wait until the bell rings before you enter the building," said Mr Snodgrass.

_____

CHALLENGE YOURSELF

Quotation marks can also be used when referring to a title. For titles, we usually add single quotation marks before and after the title. For example: I really enjoyed reading 'Matilda and the gorilla'. Add the missing quotation marks in the following sentences.

a Last year, I saw the movie Tobias and the Green Dragon with my friend Liam.

b Zoe chose Stargirl as her all-time favourite book.

Paddy Melon's shed

Paddy Melon is tidying his shed. He has laid all sorts of things out.

a hammer

pots

a dog collar

a saddle

a backpack

a billy can

a bowl

handlebars

a ladle

a saw

a tent

brakes

a cat's bowl

nails

pedals

wooden boards

a bird cage

a sleeping bag

a wooden spoon

a rabbit hutch

a puncture
repair kit

a dog lead

screws

a torch

a measuring jug

OXFORD UNIVERSITY PRESS

A comma shows a short break or pause in a sentence. Commas are used to separate words in a list. For example: *At the grocer I bought apples, peas, oranges, tomatoes and potatoes.*
Note: There is no need to use a comma when the word *and* is before the last word in a list.

1 Use the items from Paddy Melon's shed shown on page 78 to help you complete these sentences. Remember to use commas in your lists.

   a On my camping trip I will take _____
_____ and _____.

   b _____
and _____ are all parts of my bicycle.

   c To cook my soup I will need _____
_____ and _____.

   d In the box labelled 'Pets' I will put _____
_____ and _____.

   e To build my cubby I will need _____
_____ and _____.

Commas are also used to show when a reader should pause, or to separate part of the sentence from the rest of the sentence.
For example: *Mum, can I go too?*
      Over on the bench, near the sewing machine,
      stood a strange-looking elf.

2 Write commas where they belong in these sentences.

   a Melbourne the capital of Victoria is a large southern city.

   b My friend Bob who is a champion swimmer is a good tennis player.

   c Before we go in does everybody have their tickets ready?

   d *The BFG* a book written by Roald Dahl is a really funny book.

   e "Doctor can you tell me what the problem is?"

   f In a cave deep in the forest lived a terrible dragon.

Commas can change the meaning of a sentence, so be careful how you use them. Example: "I like cleaning, Dad," said Toni. "I like cleaning Dad," said Toni.

CHALLENGE YOURSELF

On a separate piece of paper or on a computer, write or type five sentences containing lists of your favourite …

   a fruits and vegetables   **b** people   **c** mammals or birds

   d TV programs or movies   **e** sports, games or hobbies

Don't forget your commas!

Knock, knock

Knock, knock

Boo.

There's no need to cry, it's only a joke.

Who's there?

Boo who?

Knock, knock

Cowsgo.

Cows don't go who, they go moo.

Who's there?

Cowsgo who?

Knock, knock

Dwayne.

Dwayne the bathtub, I'm dwowning.

Who's there?

Dwayne who?

Knock, knock

Ivor.

Ivor you let me in or I'll climb through the window.

Who's there?

Ivor who?

Knock, knock

Seymour.

Seymour if you'd open the door.

Who's there?

Seymour who?

Knock, knock

Tank.

You're welcome!

Who's there?

Tank who?

OXFORD UNIVERSITY PRESS

An apostrophe of contraction is used to show that a word has been shortened.
The apostrophe takes the place of any missing letters.
For example: *he's = he is* (the apostrophe takes the place of *i*)
                        we're = we are (the apostrophe takes the place of *a*)
                        it'll = it will (the apostrophe takes the place of *w* and *i*)

1   Write words from the 'Knock, knock' jokes on page 80 that are contractions for the
following.

a   I will _____   **b**   who is _____

c   you are _____   **d**   I am _____

e   there is _____   **f**   do not _____

g   you would _____   **h**   it is _____

2   Draw lines to match the words in Box A with their contractions in Box B.

A		B
we shall		shouldn't
they have		they'll
I have		wasn't
they will		we'll
does not		I'd
should not		doesn't
I would		they've
was not		I've

3   Copy these sentences writing the contractions in full.

a   If you don't let me in, I'll climb through the window. _____

_____

b   You'd see more if you'd open the door. _____

_____

c   There's no need to cry, it's only a joke. _____

_____

CHALLENGE YOURSELF

On a separate piece of paper or on a computer, rewrite or type the following sentences
using an apostrophe of contraction to shorten any words that can be shortened.

a   It is your turn.   **b**   Do not go in there.   **c**   I will not stay here.

d   We have done it again!   **e**   This is not mine.   **f**   They are going home now.

Crocodile and Brolga

(an Australian fable)

Crocodile was dining at his favourite waterhole. He began to cough and choke because a bone had become lodged in his throat.

"Help!" he spluttered. "Won't somebody help me please?"

Brolga, who was dancing on the plain nearby, was unsure about helping Crocodile because they had never been the best of friends.

"Help!" cried Crocodile once more. "Oh, Brolga, if only you would help me then I will reward you very well indeed. Please, oh please pull this bone from my throat."

Brolga liked the idea of a reward so she cautiously entered the waterhole and waded up to Crocodile. She thrust her head and long bill deep into the reptile's throat and pulled out the offending bone.

"Phew! That's better!" gasped Crocodile.

"Now," said Brolga, "where is the reward you have promised?"

Crocodile roared with laughter.

"You silly bird!" he said. "Your reward is that you are still alive. Few have ever lived after putting their head into my mouth."

"B...b...but," stammered Brolga, "I have been kind to you."

"Ah," smirked Crocodile, "a kindness is no kindness at all if it is merely done for a reward."

With that Crocodile gave a flip of his enormous tail, turned and disappeared into the depths of the waterhole.

OXFORD UNIVERSITY PRESS

1 Write whether each of the following sentences is a statement, a question or an exclamation.

a Won't somebody help me please? _____

b "That's better!" _____

c "Where is the reward you have promised?" _____

d Brolga liked the idea of a reward. _____

2 Write the following as contractions.

a it is _____   **b** cannot _____   **c** will not _____

d that is _____   **e** I have _____   **f** was not _____

3 Rewrite the following sentences as direct speech (don't forget to use quotation marks to show the actual words being spoken).

a Crocodile begged for help. _____

b Brolga said that she would help Crocodile. _____

_____

c Brolga asked where her reward was. _____

_____

4 Underline the conjunctions in these sentences.

a She thrust her head and long bill deep into the reptile's throat and pulled out the offending bone.

b He began to cough and choke because a bone had become lodged in his throat.

CHALLENGE YOURSELF

Write commas where they belong in the following sentences.

a Rani told us that her favourite sports were basketball soccer hockey and swimming.

b Violet indigo blue green yellow orange and red are the colours of a rainbow.

TOPIC 4: TEST YOUR GRAMMAR!

Sentences and punctuation

1 Shade the bubble next to the sentence.

- ○ in the first instance
- ○ He asked
- ○ Harry and Kate
- ○ He was over there.

2 Shade the bubble next to the sentence that is a statement.

- ○ Have you been invited?
- ○ An invitation came by email.
- ○ I'm invited!
- ○ When will my invitation arrive?

3 Shade the bubble next to the sentence that is a question.

- ○ Where are you taking that basket of fruit?
- ○ I'm taking my basket to Grandma's house.
- ○ Oops!
- ○ I've dropped it!

4 Shade the bubble next to the sentence that is an exclamation.

- ○ What are you waiting for?
- ○ It's so foggy I can't see where I'm going.
- ○ It's over there!
- ○ I wonder if Jemma has arrived home yet.

5 Shade the bubble next to the verb that agrees with the underlined subject in this sentence.

The monkeys ⬚⬚⬚⬚⬚⬚⬚⬚⬚⬚ swinging from tree to tree.

- ○ was
- ○ were
- ○ am
- ○ is

6 Shade the bubble next to the conjunction that would complete this sentence.

The police were quickly on the scene ⬚⬚⬚⬚⬚⬚⬚⬚⬚⬚ the thieves had already vanished.

- ○ and
- ○ but
- ○ so
- ○ or

OXFORD UNIVERSITY PRESS

7 Shade the bubble next to the coordinating conjunction that could join these sentences.

It had started raining heavily. We decided to take our raincoats.

○ and ○ but ○ so ○ or

8 Shade the bubble next to the sentence that is correctly punctuated.

○ Did you enjoy the movie? asked Fergie.

○ Did you enjoy the movie? "asked Fergie".

○ "Did you enjoy the movie? asked Fergie."

○ "Did you enjoy the movie?" asked Fergie.

9 Shade the bubble next to the sentence that is correctly punctuated.

○ To bake the cake you need flour, eggs, butter, currants and a little water.

○ To bake the cake you need flour eggs butter currants and, a little water.

○ To bake the cake you need flour eggs butter currants, and a little water.

○ To bake, the cake you need flour, eggs, butter, currants and a little, water.

10 Shade the bubble next to the correct contraction for **does not**.

○ do'not ○ does'nt ○ doe'snt ○ doesn't

11 Shade the bubble next to the correct contraction for **will not**.

○ willn't ○ wil'lnt ○ won't ○ wo'nt

TICK THE BOXES IF YOU UNDERSTAND

Sentences can be statements, questions or exclamations. ☐

The subject and verb of a sentence must agree. ☐

Conjunctions can be used to join words, phrases or sentences. ☐

Quotation marks show words that are actually spoken. ☐

Commas are used to separate words in a list. ☐

Apostrophes of contraction show that a word has been shortened. ☐

Gladiators

Rather than a game of football, soccer, tennis, or the Olympic Games, the sports fans of Ancient Rome <u>enjoyed</u> nothing more than a contest between gladiators.

The word *gladiator* <u>comes</u> from the Latin word *gladius*, meaning 'sword'. Most gladiators <u>were</u> slaves, prisoners of war or criminals.

Like modern sporting contests, contests between gladiators <u>were held</u> in massive stadiums before huge crowds. One of the largest of these stadiums, the Colosseum, <u>can still</u> be <u>visited</u> in Rome today.

Unlike modern sporting contests, however, gladiators usually <u>fought</u> to the death. As they <u>filed</u> past the Emperor into the Colosseum <u>to begin</u> their brutal contest, the gladiators <u>chanted</u> a final salute, "Hail Emperor! We who <u>are about to die, salute</u> you!"

However, it <u>wasn't</u> all bad for the gladiators. Those who <u>survived</u> in the arena often <u>became</u> popular heroes, much like the sports stars of today.

Information reports, like the one opposite, are usually organised into paragraphs, each starting with a topic sentence to introduce the main idea of the paragraph.

1 How many paragraphs are in the report titled 'Gladiators'?_____

2 Read the report 'Gladiators' then underline the topic sentence in each paragraph.

3 Write **first**, **second**, **third**, **fourth** or **last** to show the paragraph that describes where gladiators fight. _____

Information reports often use simple sentences to state facts. Although this report contains a lot of simple sentences with only one verb or verb group, the author has used a lot of adjectives, phrases and noun groups to build and enrich the descriptions.

4 Look at the verbs or verb groups underlined in the report opposite. How many simple sentences are in the report? _____

5 Complete these sentences with an expanded noun group from the report.

a _____ enjoyed gladiator contests.

b _____ is in Rome.

c Gladiators who survived often became _____.

Synonyms are often used in information reports to describe similarities and make the information more interesting for the reader, and antonyms are sometimes used to compare differences.

6 Find and write synonyms used in the report for each word below.

a game _____   b stadium _____

c stars _____   d start _____

7 Write an antonym from the report that is the opposite of **disliked**.

_____

CHALLENGE YOURSELF

Information reports are usually written in the present tense, unless they are about a subject that is extinct or no longer exists. Write present or past to show the correct verb tense for information reports about the following topics.

a Snakes _____   b Dinosaurs _____

What is it?

It bubbles and burbles
    and gubbles and gurgles.
It's grey and gooey,
    it's gummy and gluey.
It simmers and seethes
    and I'm sure that it breathes!
It's squishy and slushy
    and mashy and mushy.

It congeals and it clots
    and it's covered in spots.
It hisses and pops
And it plips and it plops!
Oh, where should I run?
    Oh, what can I do?
Dad's cooking again
    and he thinks that it's stew!

OXFORD UNIVERSITY PRESS

Imaginative texts such as poems are often organised in verses rather than paragraphs to allow the poet to follow a rhythmic pattern of rhyming words and rhyming lines.

1 Read the poem 'What is it?'. How many verses are in the poem?

_____

2 Write rhyming words from the poem to match the words below.

a seethes _____   b do _____

c slushy _____   d clots _____

The poet often plays with words in poems using alliteration, onomatopoeia and, occasionally, nonsense words to entertain the reader.

3 Write a line from the poem that shows alliteration.

_____

4 Find and write three nonsense words from the poem.

_____

5 Find two examples of onomatopoeia used in the poem.

_____

Adjectives (describing words) and synonyms (words with the same or similar meaning) can be used in poems to build a more interesting description for the audience.

> Remember, alliteration is a group of words that begin with the same letter or sound. For example: six silly sausages
> Onomatopoeia is when words sound like the thing they are describing. For example: hisses, pops

6 Read the poem and find synonyms for the following words.

a congeals _____   b mushy _____

7 Make a list of eight adjectives from the poem (be careful not to confuse verbs with adjectives).

_____

_____

CHALLENGE YOURSELF

Write these contractions from the poem in full.

a it's _____   b I'm _____   c Dad's _____

The grand re-opening

You're invited!

Use adjectives to describe the exciting scene.

Pronouns such as *you, we, us* refer to and include the reader.

Use exclamations to build excitement!

Use modal verbs and adverbs to persuade the audience.

12 May, 12 p.m.

After three long months, the Beechwood Skatepark upgrade is finished!

You definitely won't want to miss our fun-filled family day.

You must join us for the grand opening this Saturday afternoon!

First, Mayor Li Chan will officially open the park.

Then enjoy the *FREE SAUSAGE SIZZLE* and drinks and finally ...

GO CRAZY ON THOSE BOARDS AND BIKES!

Visuals such as photos show the reader how much fun the park will be.

Thinking and feeling verbs appeal to the readers' emotions.

Use text connectives to link and sequence parts of the text.

Let's investigate how grammar is used in persuasive texts such as the invitation opposite.

Use the guidelines to design an advertisement, poster or invitation of your own.

Use an exclamation to introduce your invitation and build excitement.

Use pronouns such as *you, we* or *us* to directly refer to and include the reader.

Use adjectives to describe the scene.

Use modal verbs and adverbs to persuade the audience.

Use thinking and feeling verbs to express opinions or appeal to the reader's emotions.

Include prepositional phrases to add details about where, when and how.

Use visuals such as illustrations to make your poster even more attractive.

Use text connectives to link and sequence the text.

UNIT 6.1   Apostrophes of possession

Mixed-up matches

The baby's tractor

The bird's spaceship

The alien's nest

The pop star's cave

The knight's lily pad

The frog's castle

The monster's cradle

The farmer's guitar

OXFORD UNIVERSITY PRESS

We use an apostrophe of possession (ownership) to show that something belongs to someone or something.

For example: *My friend's house* (the house of my friend)   *The dog's tail* (the tail belonging to the dog)

The school's library (the library of the school)

1 The things belonging to the characters on page 92 have become mixed up. Unscramble them and write the things that belong to each character using an apostrophe of possession.

For example: *The baby's cradle*

a _____   b _____

c _____   d _____

e _____   f _____

g _____   h _____

2 Rewrite these phrases using apostrophes of possession.

For example: *the claws of the tiger = the tiger's claws*

a   the beak of the eagle _____

b   the brakes of the bicycle _____

c   the pages of the book _____

d   the branches of the tree _____

e   the roar of the engine _____

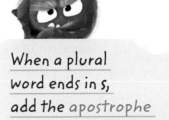

When a plural word ends in s, add the apostrophe of possession after the s. For example: the dogs' barks (more than one dog barking)

3 Tick the answer that shows the apostrophe of possession was used correctly.

a   The boy's book was lost.

The book belongs to the boy ☐ OR the boys ☐

b   The horses' hooves echoed on the cobblestones below.

The hooves belong to the horse ☐ OR the horses ☐

c   The singer's notes were perfectly in tune.

The notes belong to the singer ☐ OR the singers ☐

CHALLENGE YOURSELF

On a separate piece of paper or on a computer, rewrite or type the following sentences as newspaper headlines, showing the apostrophes of possession where necessary.

For example: *A truck crashed when its brakes failed. TRUCK'S BRAKES FAIL!*

Two trucks crashed when their brakes failed. TRUCKS' BRAKES FAIL!

a   A girl had her bag stolen.   b   Some girls had their bags stolen.

c   A quick-thinking hero saves a child.   d   Three quick-thinking heroes save a child.

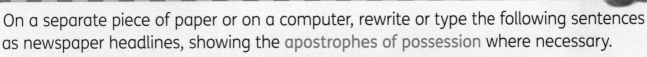

Little Redmond and Chomper the Wolf

Once upon a time a little boy called Redmond Hood was on his way through the forest. Redmond was on his way to Granny's garage with a backpack full of motorbike parts. He was halfway through the forest when he was stopped by Chomper the Wolf.

"Where are you going and what have you got in that backpack?" asked Chomper.

"I'm off to Granny's because her Harley is sick. In my pack I have some things that Granny hopes will make Harley better," said Redmond.

Ha! I have an idea, thought Chomper. If Harley is sick, then Redmond's pack must be filled with yummy food to make him feel better. If I am very clever, I might get a free feed!

Chomper jumped onto his BMX and off he raced to Granny's place.

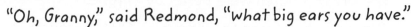

When Redmond arrived at Granny's garage he saw someone wearing grimy overalls leaning against the garage wall. Since he could see the name 'Granny' on the pocket of the overalls, Redmond presumed it was Granny wearing the overalls.

"Oh, Granny," said Redmond, "what big eyes you have."

"I'll see an optometrist tomorrow," said Chomper (disguised cleverly as Granny). "Now give me the pack, kid."

"Oh, Granny," said Redmond, "what big ears you have."

"My ear doctor appointment is next week," said Chomper. "Now hand over the goodies."

"Oh, Granny, what big, greasy, oily paws you have," said Redmond.

"All the better to swipe your bag," said Chomper and with that he grabbed Redmond's backpack and ran off into the forest.

These days, if you see a toothless wolf in the forest, don't dare mention Redmond and the crunchy backpack.

OXFORD UNIVERSITY PRESS

Some conjunctions are used to join on extra details about the main idea (main clause) in a sentence. A subordinating conjunction is used to join a main clause with a less important, subordinate clause.

For example: *Redmond went to Granny's house* **because** *her Harley was sick.*

Main clause   Subordinate clause beginning with the subordinating conjunction *because*

A clause always contains a verb. *Redmond* **went** *to Granny's house because her Harley* **was** *sick.*

Some common subordinating conjunctions are *because, when, although, since, until, while, unless, if.*

1 Read the story on page 94, then complete these sentences, adding a subordinate clause beginning with the subordinating conjunction shown in bold.

a He was halfway through the forest **when** _____.

b I'm off to Granny's **because** _____.

c **If** _____ , I might get a free feed.

d **When** _____ he saw someone wearing grimy overalls leaning against the garage wall.

e **Since** _____

_____, Redmond presumed it was Granny wearing the overalls.

Conjunctions can be used at the beginning or in the middle of a sentence.

2 Use subordinating conjunctions from the box to join the sentences below.

because   after   until

a It was a beautiful day. A cold wind started blowing. _____

_____

b The trees had been chopped down. The possums had nowhere to live. _____

_____

c We cannot go out. It is raining. _____

_____

CHALLENGE YOURSELF

Make a chart showing all the conjunctions (joining words) that you are likely to use in your writing. The information box at the top of this page may help you to get started.

It's a fact!

The largest pumpkin ever grown weighed 1190 kilograms. That's roughly the equivalent of 30 Year 4 children.

The fastest of all sea fish is the swordfish, which can reach speeds of over 100 kilometres per hour.

The world's largest crab is the Japanese spider crab. Its body measures 30 centimetres across, but from claw to claw it is 3.5 metres.

The study of where words come from is called etymology.

A funambulist is a tightrope walker.

The study of mountains is called orology.

When cooking in a submarine that is underwater, the ship's cooks use peanut oil because under normal conditions it does not smoke like other oils.

Sir Joseph Banks was a botanist on Captain James Cook's journey to Australia in 1770. He gave his name to one of our country's most popular native plants — the banksia.

According to podiatrists, the average pair of feet will walk about 190 000 kilometres in a lifetime.

OXFORD UNIVERSITY PRESS

A **prefix** comes at the beginning of a word. It changes the meaning of the original word.

1   Write words from the facts on page 96 that begin with these **prefixes**.

   a   kilo- (meaning one thousand) _____

   b   centi- (meaning one hundred) _____

   c   sub- (meaning under) _____

2   The **suffix** *-ist* means 'one who can'. The **suffix** *-ology* means 'the study of'. Find words in the facts on page 96 that mean the following.

   a   the study of mountains _____

   b   one who studies botany _____

   c   one who specialises in the treatment of feet

   _____

   d   one who walks on a tightrope _____

> A **suffix** is added to the end of a word to change the meaning of the word.
>
> For example: *art + ist* (meaning, one who can) = artist (meaning, one who can do art)

CHALLENGE YOURSELF

Match the words in box A with their meanings in Box B

A	B
subterranean	one who studies the Earth and its structure
cyclist	a title that comes under a main title
geologist	under the ground
subtitle	one hundred years
motorist	one who rides a bicycle
subway	a supposedly one-hundred-footed insect
century	an underground passageway
centipede	one who drives a road vehicle

Tweedledee and Tweedledum

They were standing under a tree, each with an arm round the other's neck, and Alice knew which was which in a moment, because one of them had 'DUM' embroidered on his collar, and the other 'DEE'. "I suppose they've each got 'TWEEDLE' round at the back of the collar," she said to herself.

They stood so still that she quite forgot they were alive, and she was just looking round to see if the word 'TWEEDLE' was written at the back of each collar, when she was startled by a voice coming from the one marked 'DUM'.

"If you think we're wax-works," he said, "you ought to pay, you know. Wax-works weren't made to be looked at for nothing. Nohow!"

"Contrariwise," added the one marked 'DEE', "if you think we're alive, you ought to speak."

"I'm sure I'm very sorry," was all Alice could say; for the words of the old song kept ringing through her head like the ticking of a clock, and she could hardly help saying them out loud:—

> Tweedledum and Tweedledee
>
> Agreed to have a battle;
>
> For Tweedledum said Tweedledee
>
> Had spoiled his nice new rattle.

> Just then flew down a monstrous crow
>
> As black as a tar-barrel;
>
> Which frightened both the heroes so,
>
> They quite forgot their quarrel.

from *Alice Through the Looking-Glass* by Lewis Carroll

OXFORD UNIVERSITY PRESS

1 Write apostrophes of possession where they belong in these phrases.

a the others neck

b the crows feathers

c Alices song

d both boys names (careful!)

e the childrens game

2 Use the story on page 98 and conjunctions to help you rewrite these sentences as one longer, more interesting sentence.

They were standing under a tree, each with an arm round the other's neck. Alice knew which was which in a moment. One of them had 'DUM' embroidered on his collar and the other 'DEE'.

_____

_____

_____

_____

_____

3 Change the following verbs to happening verbs by adding the suffix -ing.

a say _____

b ring _____

c tick _____

d come _____

e drop _____

f battle _____

4 Add the prefixes anti-, sub- or bi- to the following words to form new words and then write a definition for each.

a _____marine _____

b _____cycle _____

c _____clockwise _____

CHALLENGE YOURSELF

Use the subordinating conjunctions in the box to help you complete the following sentences in your own words.

because   after   until

a Alice could tell the boys apart _____

b They were agreeing to have a battle _____

c We waited patiently _____

BOOK 4: TEST YOUR GRAMMAR!

1 Shade the bubble next to the common noun.

- ○ blue
- ○ jump
- ○ ship
- ○ quietly

2 Shade the bubble next to the correct plural noun for **life**.

- ○ lives
- ○ lifies
- ○ livies
- ○ lifes

3 Shade the bubble next to the proper noun.

- ○ rocket
- ○ Rockhampton
- ○ rock
- ○ rocking

4 Shade the bubble next to the concrete noun.

- ○ happiness
- ○ love
- ○ anger
- ○ battle

5 Shade the bubble next to the abstract noun.

- ○ laugh
- ○ laughter
- ○ happy
- ○ happiness

6 Shade the bubble below the adjective in this sentence.

The valiant gladiators fought bravely before the Emperor.

    ○   ○   ○   ○

7 Shade the bubble next to the adverb.

- ○ gentle
- ○ gently
- ○ gentlemen
- ○ gentleman

OXFORD UNIVERSITY PRESS

8 Shade the bubble next to the doing verb.

◯ wrote ◯ house ◯ slowly ◯ Maya

9 Shade the bubble below the saying verb in this sentence.

'Are we there yet?' moaned the children in the back seat.

◯ ◯ ◯ ◯

10 Shade the bubble next to the word that is a preposition in this phrase.

over the rickety bridge

◯ over ◯ the ◯ rickety ◯ bridge

11 Shade the bubble under the word that is a pronoun in this sentence.

The children entered the darkened room, their torches ready.

◯ ◯ ◯ ◯

12 Shade the bubble next to the prefix that means **under**.

◯ centi- ◯ sub- ◯ kilo- ◯ anti-

13 Shade the bubble next to the correct contraction of **is not**.

◯ isnt ◯ isnt' ◯ is'nt ◯ isn't

Complete the 'Time to reflect' section on the next two pages.

TIME TO REFLECT

Tick each box when you are confident that you understand and can use the grammar listed when you write.

	Understand	Use
I select specific common, proper or abstract nouns to represent people, places, things and ideas.	☐	☐
I choose suitable nouns to fit the topic of my writing or to represent different characters. For example: **girl, princess**	☐	☐
I use adjectives to describe characters and settings to make my writing more interesting.	☐	☐
I know how to expand noun groups with articles and adjectives to make my writing more meaningful to the reader.	☐	☐
I use thinking and feeling verbs to express opinions.	☐	☐
I use modal verbs such as **could, would, should** and **must** to express opinions or persuade my audience.	☐	☐
I choose suitable action, saying or relating verbs to report facts or entertain the reader.	☐	☐
I can use present, past and future tense verbs correctly.	☐	☐
I use adverbs and prepositional phrases to make interesting sentences with details about where, when, how or why something happens.	☐	☐
I use antonyms (opposites) and synonyms (similar meaning) to help describe and compare people, places, things or ideas.	☐	☐
I use paragraphs to organise my writing into logical bundles.	☐	☐
I use topic sentences to introduce the main idea in each paragraph.	☐	☐
I use pronouns that agree with the noun to which they refer. For example: **Evie/she, the boys/they**	☐	☐

OXFORD UNIVERSITY PRESS

	Understand	**Use**
I know how to use text connectives to link paragraphs or sentences in time or sequence. For example: **first, then, later, finally**	☐	☐
I know how to write statements, questions and exclamations.	☐	☐
I know how to use the coordinating conjunctions **and, but, so** and **or** to make a compound sentence.	☐	☐
I know the difference between simple sentences and compound sentences.	☐	☐
I understand that the subject and verb in a sentence must agree.	☐	☐
I recognise how quotation marks are used in quoted (direct) speech.	☐	☐
I understand the difference between quoted (direct) and reported (indirect) speech.	☐	☐
I use commas in lists correctly most of the time.	☐	☐
I understand that an apostrophe of contraction can be used to show where a letter is missing in a shortened word.	☐	☐

GLOSSARY

adjective	A describing word: *red, old, large, round, three*
adverb	A word that usually adds meaning to a verb to tell when, where or how something happened: *slowly, immediately, soon, here* modal adverb (shows degree of certainty): *definitely, probably*
alliteration	A group of words that begin with or contain the same sound: *six silly sausages*
antonym	An opposite: *full/empty, sitting/standing, front/back*
apostrophe of contraction	A punctuation mark that shows where a letter is missing in a shortened word: *isn't, we'll, I'm, shouldn't*
apostrophe of possession	A punctuation mark that shows ownership: *Bob's hat, the man's car, the boys' backpacks*
clause	A group of words that contain a verb and its subject
comma	A punctuation mark used to separate items in a list, to show a short pause or to separate a main clause and a subordinate clause: *Mum, can I go? When I leave, I will take some apples, bananas, oranges and cherries.*
coordinating conjunction	A joining word used to join two simple sentences or main ideas: *and, but, or, so*
exclamation	A sentence that shows a raised voice or strong feeling: *Look out! Hey you! Don't look yet!*
noun	A word that names people, places, animals, things or ideas. Nouns can be: abstract nouns (things that cannot be seen or touched): *happiness, idea* common nouns (names of ordinary things): *hat, toys, pet, mouse, clock, bird*

OXFORD UNIVERSITY PRESS

concrete nouns (things that can be seen or touched): *book, pet, boy, girl*

proper nouns (special names): *Max, Perth, Friday, March, Easter, Australia*

technical nouns (sometimes called scientific nouns): *oxygen, carbon dioxide*

noun group	A group of words, often including an article, an adjective and a noun, built around a main noun: *the strange, old house*.
onomatopoeia	Words that sound like the thing they are describing: *Bang! Crash!*
paragraph	A section of text containing a number of sentences about a particular point. Each paragraph starts on a new line.
phrase	A group of words (without a verb) that adds details about when, where, how, why: *in the car, after lunch, with a spoon, for Olivia*
plural	More than one: *chairs, dishes, boxes, cities, donkeys, loaves, foci*
preposition	A word that usually begins a phrase: *on, in, over, under, before, near, with*
prepositional phrase	A phrase formed when a preposition is followed by a noun or noun group: *in bed, on the weekend*
pronoun	A word that can take the place of a noun to represent a person, place or thing: *he, she, I, it, they, we, us, me, they, them, mine* possessive pronoun: *mine, ours, his, hers, yours, theirs*
pun	A word play in which a word or phrase is used in a different way to make what is being written humorous: *I used to be a tailor, but I found the work was just so-so.*
question	A sentence that asks something: *Is Tock hiding under the bed?*
quoted (direct) speech	The words that someone actually says. Quoted speech uses quotation marks at the start and end of the actual words spoken.
reported (indirect) speech	The words reporting what someone else has said.

sentence	A group of words that makes sense, and includes a subject and at least one verb. A simple sentence has one main idea or main clause and one verb or verb group: *The birds **were sitting** on the fence.* A compound sentence uses *and, but, so* or *or* to join two main ideas or main clauses. A compound sentence has two verbs or verb groups: *Some birds **were sitting** on the fence and a cat **was lurking** below.*
spoonerism	A word play in which the first letters or sounds of words are mixed up: *Wave the sails! (Save the whales!)*
statement	A sentence that states facts or gives opinions: *The horses ran around the paddock. I like ice cream.*
subject	The noun or noun group naming who or what a sentence is about.
subordinating conjunction	A joining word used to join a main clause and one or more subordinate clauses: *because, since, when, if*
synonym	A word that means the same or nearly the same as another word: *shouts/yells, thin/skinny*
text connective	A signpost word or group of words that tells how the text is developing – generally used to link two sentences or paragraphs.
topic sentence	A sentence, usually placed at the start of a paragraph, that introduces the main point being made in the paragraph.
verb	A word that tells us what is happening in a sentence. Verbs can be: doing verbs: *walked, swam* modal verbs (telling how sure we are about doing something): *should, could, would, may, might, must, can, will, shall* thinking and feeling verbs: *know, like* relating verbs: *am, is, are, had* saying verbs: *said, asked*
verb group	A group of words built around a head word that is a verb: *might have been wondering*
verb tense	The form a verb takes to show when an action takes place – in the present, past or future: *runs/is running, thought/was thinking, will help*

OXFORD UNIVERSITY PRESS